An Introduction t␣ Graphics Concepts: from Pixels to Pictures

Sun Microsystems, Inc.

Addison-Wesley Publishing Company, Inc.
Reading, Massachusetts   Menlo Park, California   New York
Don Mills, Ontario   Wokingham, England   Amsterdam
Bonn   Sydney   Singapore   Tokyo   Madrid   San Juan
Paris   Seoul   Milan   Mexico City   Taipei

The OPEN LOOK Graphical User Interface was developed by Sun Microsystems, Inc., for its users and licensees. Sun acknowledges the pioneering efforts of Xerox in researching and developing the concept of visual or graphical user interfaces for the computer industry. Sun holds a non-exclusive license from Xerox to the Xerox Graphical User Interface, which license also covers Sun's licensees.

Sun, the Sun logo, and Sun Microsystems are registered trademarks of Sun Microsystems, Inc. Open Windows is a trademark of Sun Microsystems, Inc.

OPEN LOOK is a registered trademark of UNIX Systems Laboratories.

POSTSCRIPT is a trademark of Adobe Systems Incorporated.

The X Window System is a product of the Massachusetts Institute of Technology.

Copyright © 1991 by Sun Microsystems, Inc.

Sponsoring Editor: Carole McClendon
Cover Design: Hannus Design Associates
Set in 10-point Palatino in FrameMaker™
ISBN 0-201-56789-X

1 2 3 4 5 6 7 8 9-AL-9594939291
First printing, June 1991

Contents

An Introduction to Computer Graphics Concepts

Preface

An Introduction to Computer Graphics Concepts: from Pixels to Pictures is a fundamental guide to computer graphics terminology and concepts. It presents a concise description of the steps involved in creating and modifying pictures on a graphics workstation, without delving into the complex underlying mathematics. Additionally, the book provides an overview of the many creative, technical, and scientific uses for computer graphics and discusses the hardware capabilities required to achieve various levels of graphics sophistication.

Audience

This book is for anyone who wants to learn about computer graphics but does not want to read a highly technical text. It will be especially helpful to users and programmers new to the complex computer graphics environment who need an accessible overview of concepts and terminology. Finally, anyone who is considering the purchase of a graphics system or software should find this book an excellent resource for making informed decisions.

How to Use This Book

This book is organized into chapters that describe the major tasks and events involved in graphics computing. Those who choose to read the chapters sequentially will find an intuitive order to the material. Others may wish to use the book as a reference text. Specific concepts can be located in the table of contents, the glossary, and the index. Important terms are highlighted in **bold** throughout the text, and terms used in the glossary are *italicized* if they are also defined under their own names.

Brief Overview

Chapter 1, "Who Needs Computer Graphics?" provides a brief overview of the practical uses of computer graphics technology, and an introduction to the topics covered in the remainder of the book.

Chapter 2, "The Computer Graphics Environment," describes the components of the graphics system as well as the roles of the people who make graphics computing possible.

Chapter 3, "Displaying Graphics," introduces raster graphics display technology, from pixels and frame buffers to the mechanics involved in displaying colors and complex pictures.

Chapter 4, "Graphics Fundamentals," describes the basic elements used to produce graphical objects, and introduces two-dimensional and three-dimensional graphics.

Chapter 5, "Making Pictures," discusses the basic design considerations involved in developing graphical applications, and introduces many useful algorithms for creating pictures.

Chapter 6, "Surface Rendering and Realism," discusses how object surfaces can be rendered with lighting models to produce complex and realistic effects. Additionally, it introduces advanced techniques such as ray tracing and radiosity.

Chapter 7, "Modifying and Viewing Pictures," describes the basic transformations that can be performed on graphical objects, and provides an overview of the "viewing pipeline" in both two and three dimensions.

Chapter 8, "Graphics Libraries," provides a look at how graphics libraries handle picture updates, and introduces several industry standard graphics libraries.

Chapter 9, "Image Processing and Visualization," introduces several imaging technologies and discusses important graphics topics, such as scientific visualization.

An Introduction to Computer Graphics Concepts

Chapter 10, "Applications," provides an overview of some of the many technical and creative fields that are using computer graphics technology, and discusses their software needs.

Chapter 11, "Performance Metrics," discusses the hardware needs of the application areas introduced in Chapter 10. Additionally, this chapter looks at the ways in which graphics system performance is measured, and introduces the development of standards for performance measurement.

The Glossary defines many important graphics-related terms.

The Bibliography provides a list of books and articles that can serve as a reading list for those who would like to learn more about the topics covered in the book.

A Color Plate section is included. The Color Plates are referenced throughout the book, as the topics illustrated in this section are discussed.

Acknowledgments

Jayna Pike wrote this book with technical assistance from Bob Mitton and W. Dean Stanton. Donald T. Weaver created the line drawings. Brian Yen produced the computer-generated art that appears on the front cover. William Pratt provided the halftone images and technical help for the image processing section. Brian Croll, Will Shelton, and Ingrid Van Den Hoogen brought enthusiasm and computer graphics expertise to the project and helped make it into a book.

We gratefully acknowledge the following people who provided assistance with screen illustrations, technical content, readability, and moral support: Kathy Abelson, Robert Aronoff, Bruce Bartlett, Todd Basche, Pierre Bedard, Tony Cussary, Michael Deering, Gary Ebersole, Ed Falk, Jim Fitzpatrick, Bill Gogesch, Ken Hauck, Brian Herzog, Marty Hess, John Hevelin, Lori Ingle, Virginia Kean, Mike Lavelle, Patrick Maillot, Ken Marks, Andrea Marra, Bob McKee, Donna McMillan, Tom McReynolds, Steve Misawa, Scott Nelson, Sunita Neti, Ralph Nichols, Charles Poynton, Ruth Ramberg, John Ravella, Irma Rodriguez, Debra Ronsvalle, Kevin Rushforth, Doug Schiff, Ken Schneider, Evelyn Spire, Niraj Swarup, Lauren Swingle, Geri Younggren, and Audrey Zenner Billet.

Many thanks to Mary Cavaliere, Diane Freed, Joanne Clapp Fullagar, Rachel Guichard, Carole McClendon, and Jean Seal at Addison-Wesley for their contributions to this effort.

Who Needs Computer Graphics?

Computer graphics, once inaccessible to all but highly technical individuals with excellent financial resources, is now affordable and accessible for many users—from the cartoonist who wants to create animation frames more efficiently, to the scientist who wants to analyze complex and abstract data using an intuitive graphical format. Computer graphics enables users in a wide variety of creative, technical, and scientific fields to simplify the presentation of complex information, to synthesize vast amounts of data into crisp graphical formats for analysis, and to expedite the design phase of product development.

The uses for computer graphics are so diverse that they may seem to have little in common. However, three commonalities exist throughout all computer graphics environments. First, the graphical medium enables us to communicate ideas visually. Whether the output originates from scientific data, aerodynamics testing, design specifications, sales projections, or creative inspiration, graphics provides a visually meaningful method of presenting information and ideas.

Second, computer graphics pictures are **computer-generated**. Whether the goal is to design an automobile, map the terrain for a flight simulator, or show exploded views of tiny mechanical parts, the user provides the ideas and information, and the computer uses these data to construct the visual representation.

This leads into the third distinction: computer graphics is **interactive**. Although in many cases it is possible to create the same images on paper, the finality of paper images is inherently limiting. With computer graphics, the user can lay the ground work for designs and simulations and then test the effects of various changes on the initial model. The computer graphics system quickly incorporates the modifications or new testing data, and provides the results in a visually comprehensible format. These interactive features also enable the user to move the pictures into new locations and to rotate them to view the same objects from different angles.

Computer graphics empowers us to try new solutions and to test our ideas before they are "carved in stone." It enables us to off-load much of the hard work onto sophisticated state-of-the art computer graphics workstations, thus freeing us to explore alternatives and check accuracy. Most importantly, computer graphics gives us a powerful interactive tool for creating visual representations of our ideas.

Image Processing

In many environments, image processing and computer graphics are companion technologies. In contrast to computer graphics, image-processing data are not generated by the computer, but are externally generated images that are scanned or digitized to be displayed on a computer. Typically originating as photographs, satellite data, or medical images such as X-rays, these images can be processed on the computer graphics workstation. This technology is useful in fields as diverse as cartography, urban planning, weather forecasting, and medical treatment planning. Many users combine image processing and computer graphics technologies to better suit their particular needs. Although this book is primarily devoted to the discussion of computer graphics, it also discusses image processing.

The remainder of this chapter explores several realms in which computer graphics, image processing, or both are serving users' needs.

Graphics in Design

In environments such as mechanical design, circuit board design, civil engineering, and architectural design, sophisticated graphics software tools enable users to work more efficiently than with traditional methods. These tools enable the user to create designs efficiently and interactively, to share drawings with other users electronically, to store and access drawings from a database, and to update and modify drawings as plans change or as clients request new features.

An Introduction to Computer Graphics Concepts

Traditionally, a design for a new piece of equipment was drafted on paper and often had to be drawn more than once if the initial efforts revealed problems. The second phase of the design process generally included production of a costly prototype. Because of its ability to handle complex picture data, computer graphics is often a much more expedient and less expensive solution. Complex diagrams can be constructed, altered, and tested prior to manufacturing. For instance, computer chip and circuit board designers often use software packages that enable them to run the final design through a series of tests to determine the product's viability.

Figure 1-1 illustrates an electronic circuit board design created on a graphics system.

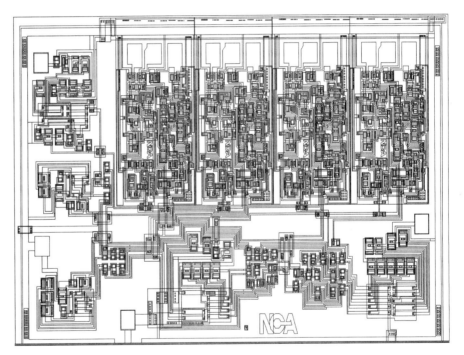

Figure 1-1   A computer chip created with electronic design software.

Because of the complexity of some of these designs, it is virtually impossible to visually inspect them for problems, so the inspection and testing processes are automated on the computer. Thus, computer graphics enables designers to accelerate the design process, improve product design with on-line refining and testing tools, and shorten time to market.

In the Media

Television is a common medium for computer graphics. Animated children's cartoons and the "flying logos" used in news and sports programs are several examples of the prevalent use of animated computer graphics. Other media environments use graphics for production of hard-copy advertising and for creating brochures and other publications. This eliminates the expense and turn-around time involved in sending ad copy out to special design firms. Many newspaper, magazine, and newsletter publishers are using on-line publishing software as well. The software provides interactive tools for creating graphical layouts and designs, and thereby increases the designer's efficiency.

Professional illustrators, too, are discovering productivity gains with computer graphics. Medical illustrators, technical illustrators, and graphic artists have a great variety of software tools and graphics systems from which to choose.

In Science and Medicine

Scientists generate voluminous amounts of data in diverse research environments such as atmospheric and climatic research, geological exploration, and astro-physics, but the data are opaque to us when they remain in numerical form. Visual representations are inherently more meaningful than a multitude of numbers. Computer graphics provides a way to remove the bottleneck, and to enable scientists, engineers, and analysts to reassemble the data into meaningful visual information.

"Visualization" is one of the buzzwords of the nineties. With modern graphics workstations, we can visualize environments that, in the real world, are inaccessible. Computer graphics and image processing virtually enable us to visit places that are otherwise too distant, too small, too hot, too cold, or too dangerous for human beings. Distant galaxies, the insides of blood vessels, lava flows, nuclear reactors, and the earth hundreds of feet beneath the surface are just a few examples of objects and environments that can be recreated or simulated with computer pictures.

In medicine, computer graphics enables physicians to determine the locations of tumors and deformities with non-invasive techniques. X-rays, CAT-scans, and volume representations constructed from these sources enable the radiologist and surgeon to view problem areas and to plan the patient's treatment with precision.

An Introduction to Computer Graphics Concepts

Other scientific environments, such as coal and oil exploration, smog testing, reforestation planning, crop analysis, and seismic interpretation, make use of computer graphics to analyze gathered data from tests and satellite photographs. Computer-generated models and simulations enable researchers to test theories and visualize events, such as the movement of tectonic plates and the effect of various influences on the environment. Weather forecasters make use of the combined technologies of computer graphics and image processing by overlaying satellite images of weather fronts entering a geographic region on graphical map grids with familiar state boundaries. Demographic researchers use databases of census and demographic information and graphically-generated maps to determine the best locations for shopping centers and to advise local authorities of the best locations for hospitals and fire stations.

In summary, computer graphics is much more than pretty pictures and much more than an elitist field for those who can afford it. Graphics programs range in sophistication from paint programs and illustration packages for cartoonists and illustrators to high-end modeling programs for medical and pharmaceutical researchers. Computer graphics, in all of its forms—animated cartoons, business publications, medical solutions, and so on—is playing an increasing role in the way we view our surroundings and the way we do business in the modern world.

In order to create and process images with computers, the applications for computer graphics that we have discussed require special sets of ingredients. Chapter 2 introduces the components and terminology of the computer graphics system and software that make graphics computing possible.

The Computer Graphics Environment

This chapter introduces the computer graphics environment, from the computer hardware and software to the programmer who creates graphics tools for the user. Topics include:

- The graphics system

- The application

- The application developer

- The graphics library

- The application database

- Hardware and software interaction

- Peripheral devices

- Networked graphics

The Graphics System

The graphics system is a collection of hardware devices and software programs that interact to produce graphical images. It includes the graphics workstation, which is the hardware that computes and displays graphical pictures, and the software that enables the user to create and manipulate the pictures. The hardware devices represent the potential of the graphics system: they are the power that makes it possible to produce images. The software represents the orchestration of that potential: it uses the power of the hardware to create images that are meaningful to the viewer. This section introduces the graphics system—the variety of hardware devices and software systems that enable users to create graphical images with computers.

The Graphics Workstation

The graphics workstation is a set of hardware devices that generally includes a monitor with special display memory for producing complex pictures, a keyboard and mouse, one or more processors (such as a CPU and a specialized graphics computing device), and storage devices—such as a disk—which may reside inside the primary computer package with the processor or in a separate unit that stands next to the desk. Figure 2-1 illustrates one of several possible arrangements, in which the processing hardware resides on the desktop.

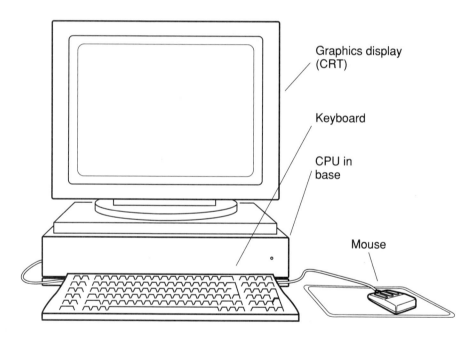

Graphics display
(CRT)

Keyboard

CPU in
base

Mouse

Figure 2-1   A graphics workstation.

If not included locally in the workstation setup, the storage space may reside remotely on another machine, to be accessed by the graphics workstation over a **network** (see "Graphics on the Network" later in this chapter).

An Introduction to Computer Graphics Concepts

There are several advantages to running graphics programs in a workstation environment, rather than on a personal computer or a terminal connected to a mainframe. First, the workstation vendor typically provides all of the hardware as well as essential software—such as windowing software and a graphics library—as a complete package. (The windowing software and the graphics library are discussed shortly.) All of these elements are integrated into one graphics system setup in advance of purchase.

Second, because of the integration of the system, the software is optimized to run efficiently on the hardware. Additionally, support for the entire package is often available through one vendor, as opposed to separate vendors for separate products (usually with the exception of the graphics **application** software, which is provided by an **independent software vendor**, or **ISV**).

Third, graphics workstations tend to be considerably more powerful than personal computers. Many graphics programs are very sophisticated and compute-intensive, requiring powerful hardware to run efficiently. The faster and more specialized the graphical components of the computer, the faster the graphics. ("The Graphics Accelerator," later in this chapter, introduces these specialized components.)

Fourth, the workstation setup is priced competitively with and is more flexible than environments involving a series of terminals that access data and storage from a **mainframe** computer. Although the cost of terminals is low, when a share of the mainframe expense is added to their purchase price, their cost is comparable to workstation costs. Unlike terminals, each graphics workstation, whether running on a network or as a **stand-alone** machine, has its own compute power, can be equipped with its own graphics software, and can receive its own upgrades in hardware performance.

Finally, the large-sized monitors available for graphics workstations are capable of clearly displaying the output of programs with many features and graphical tools at once. Complex graphics software, such as a program that emulates a design environment (a drafting table, for example), benefits greatly from the large area on the workstation display.

The Graphical Display

The graphical display is a device very much like a television (or video monitor) that displays graphical images as well as the visual **interfaces** to other programs, such as electronic mail and word processing software. Graphical displays are often **cathode-ray tubes**, or **CRTs**. Inside the CRT, an electron gun emits a controlled beam of electrons that strikes the screen surface from within, illuminating a **phosphorous** coating on the screen.

Figure 2-2 illustrates the electron gun and the beam inside the graphics monitor striking the phosphor surface.

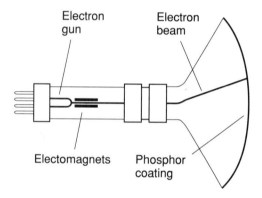

Figure 2-2   The CRT's electron gun.

Color monitors display images in combinations of three **primary** colors: red, green, and blue. The method of combining colors for computer graphics display is based on a model of how colored light mixes. This model, called the **RGB color model** (discussed in "Multi-Bit Displays," in Chapter 3), involves an **additive** process, which means that portions of the three primary colors are added together to create the colors used to produce and display an image. The RGB color model is used to match what we recognize as distinct color hues with colors the CRT is capable of producing. The basis for the selection of these three colors as the primaries for mixing other colors is beyond the scope of this book. However, it helps to understand one premise of color theory: the eye has three color sensors that have peak sensitivity to red, green, and blue light.

Phosphor Dots and Pixels

The phosphor coating on the CRT is composed of tiny dots. Each of the dots is a triad of phosphors that emits red, green, and blue light. The electron gun in the color CRT shines a three-part beam through a **mask** that essentially shields portions of the phosphor from the spray of electrons. This helps to focus the beams so that each beam strikes only one color on the phosphor triad. Figure 2-3 illustrates this process.

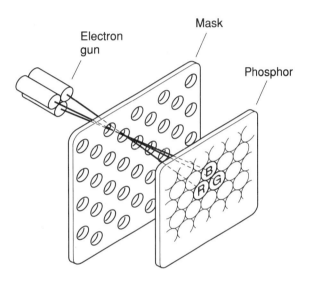

Figure 2-3   One phosphor triad illuminated by the three-part beam of the electron gun.

Producing color on the display involves adjusting the intensity of the electron beams to control the amount of light emitted by the colored phosphors. Because the phosphor triads are very small and close together, the observer's eye blends the colors and sees the appropriate color result. The phosphor triads are grouped into small dots visible on the graphics display screen. These larger dots, known as picture elements, or **pixels**, are used to produce images and text. A display controller in the hardware selects a color value for each pixel and regulates the intensities of the electron beams. The final result is an image composed of dot patterns in a rectangular grid called a **raster**.

It is usually possible to see the tiny red, green, and blue dots on a television monitor if the displayed image is primarily white. Graphics workstations typically have better **resolution** than television monitors, so the pixels are even smaller and more numerous than those on a regular television screen. Resolution is the number of pixels in the horizontal and vertical dimensions of the screen, but this must take into account the screen's size: two displays with the same number of pixels differ in resolution if they are not the same size.

Scan Conversion and Raster Refresh

Determining the color, monochrome or gray-scale value of each of the pixels involves a process called **scan conversion**. The picture to be drawn on the screen must be **sampled** to determine its placement on the display device in pixels. The sampling process tests many points along the lines or across the surfaces of each graphical object and stores these values in the **frame buffer** (the display memory).

The graphics display's electron beam sweeps across the display surface in a scan-line pattern, along each row of pixels. The value for each pixel on the display screen is obtained from the frame buffer and converted from digital to analog (voltage) form to select the electron beam intensity. As the electron beam scans rapidly along the scan-line rows, its electrons strike the phosphor with the intensity dictated by the frame buffer's pixel values.

Because the phosphor glows very briefly, the display must be **refreshed**. To refresh the raster screen, the electron beam sweeps sequentially across the many scan lines to illuminate the phosphor coating corresponding to all of the selected pixels throughout the time they are displayed. The rate of refresh depends upon the particular hardware, but typically the beam refreshes the raster at rates between 30 and 100 times per second. Displays with a refresh rate of less than 30 frames per second appear to flicker, because the phosphor begins to fade before it can be refreshed.

Note that there are several methods of scanning the raster. With the **interlaced** method, the electron beam scans every other row of pixels, and then returns to the top of the display and scans the remaining rows. The **non-interlaced** method, which is generally preferred for graphical displays, scans each row of pixels in a single refresh, tracing the whole picture at once. The latter method requires a greater effective scan rate—approximately 60 cycles per second through the whole raster as opposed to approximately 30 per second.

Graphics Computing

Computer processors are engines that interpret and transform the ideas stored as programs (software) into some action. The computing hardware of a graphics system (often called the **platform**) may include multiple processors that perform a variety of tasks. The graphics system's software subsystems define the sets of actions that the processors need to perform. For instance, many of these actions handle communications between window systems, operating systems, and graphics programs.

All of the information that makes it possible to draw and display computer pictures is represented in numerical **data** and must be managed by one or more of the graphics system's processors. Computer-generated pictures consist of data describing the geometry and placement of an object as well as the object's **attributes**, such as color, and all other information required to place an image on the display surface. For pictures that have been generated by another source (a photograph, for example) and then displayed on the CRT, the data describe how the placement of the many points of color (or gray values) on the screen represent the image. The processors must handle all of these data as pictures are drawn, manipulated, and displayed.

The CPU

The CPU, the workstation's general purpose processor, performs operations of all varieties, including calculations on picture and text data. It manages all user input, from the keyboard or other input devices as well as output to the display or to a printer and the mathematics of hardware/software communications. Because this great amount and variety of traffic in the computer can belabor compute-intensive operations, such as complex graphics programs, the workstation may include a second processor, called the **graphics accelerator**.

The Graphics Accelerator

In sophisticated graphics systems there is often at least one specialized graphics accelerator that is dedicated to improving the speed of picture drawing. The accelerator's specialized processing relieves the CPU and graphics software of the burden of graphics display processing so that the entire graphics system functions more efficiently.

There are a number of possible configurations for the CPU and accelerator. In a general case, the accelerator performs as a slave to the CPU, processing the data the CPU passes to it. For instance, it usually performs the scan conversion that transforms the picture data into pixels on the screen.

Several levels of graphics acceleration are available for graphics workstations. Whether or not acceleration is necessary, and the amount of acceleration needed, depends directly on the level of graphics sophistication desired. At a minimum, an accelerator off-loads tasks that the CPU would have to do, improving the efficiency of the CPU's operations. Increased levels of acceleration can dramatically improve the efficiency of user interaction as well as the speed of graphics programs—such as animation—that involve a lot of movement, thus making large demands on the computer. Acceleration always comes at a cost; thus, there are trade-offs to make in deciding upon the amount of hardware support to purchase with a graphics system. (See "Price/Performance Trade-Offs" in Chapter 11.)

The Windowing Environment

Most of today's graphics workstations use windowing technology. Windows operate like separate displays: each window on the graphics monitor can run its own graphics program. This technology enables the graphics user to run a variety of programs simultaneously. The user can usually stack the windows in any order and modify each to a chosen size. To keep the workstation free of clutter, the user can close windows that are not in use. On many systems, closed windows becomes program **icons**, which are graphical symbols— usually about the size of a postage stamp—that represent the program's function and that can be re-opened for further use. Figure 2-4 illustrates a window system running an application and several other windows.

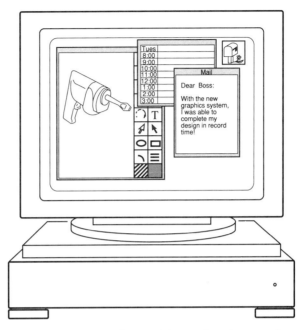

Figure 2-4   A window system on the graphics workstation, running multiple programs.

The window system is a complex software system that is responsible for managing (in coordination with the computer's **operating system**) the multiple programs running on the graphics system. For example, if the user runs a design program, a daily calendar, electronic mail, and a desktop publishing package, each in separate windows, the windowing software and operating system must handle each of these communications and their related events in the hardware.

The Mouse

Because the workstation display can have several working windows at any given time, it is important for the user to be able to point to various places on the screen and to select active work areas. The **mouse**, a small hand-sized device, is the most common pointing device.

The mouse is usually connected to the graphics workstation by a small cable and typically sits on a pad next to the workstation. An electronic eye or a small rolling ball beneath it provides direction and movement information to the computer. On the top of the mouse, one or more buttons act as indicators for the user to make selections. When the user moves the mouse, a message is sent to a **device driver** (software code that manages interactions between software and hardware), that updates the position of a special **pointer** (such as an arrow) on the screen. This pointer is often called a **cursor**, as is a text marker that moves one character at a time in a text window. To avoid confusion, we will use the term *pointer* for the marker corresponding to mouse movement. Figure 2-5 illustrates the mouse next to the workstation and the pointer in a text window.

Figure 2-5   The mouse and its corresponding pointer in the application window.

The user can choose a window or application by moving the mouse button and corresponding pointer, and can use the mouse buttons to "point and click" to make selections. Selecting a window is a matter of moving the mouse across its pad until the pointer appears in the chosen window. In graphics programs, the point-and-click operation can be used for such things as changing a color and moving an object to a new location.

The Graphical User Interface

The window system is the user's interface to the computer's tools and programs, and must be intuitive and easy to use. The "look and feel" of the window system and program tools is called a **graphical user interface**, or **GUI** (sometimes pronounced *gooey*). Because many of the user's traditional tasks—such as typing, editing, storing files, sending mail, and printing documents—now occur on a workstation, GUI programs usually seek to resemble their familiar counterparts, such as file folders, mail boxes, and pushpins. Color Plate 1 illustrates two graphics applications running in the OPEN LOOK® graphical user interface environment, developed by Sun Microsystems, Inc. and AT&T.

Three common methods for accessing utilities in graphics applications are **buttons**, **sliders**, and pull-down or pop-up **menus**. These tools enable the user to manipulate aspects of the picture quickly and easily. The pull-down and pop-up menus offer the graphics user options such as a list of geometric shapes to be used in object construction or a list of previously created and stored objects. The user can click on a button or place the pointer on a slider and adjust it by sliding the mouse right or left. Buttons generally indicate on/off operations. Typical buttons might start or stop rotation of a graphical object or switch from a transparent object construction to a solid surface. Sliders indicate selections in a range, such as the amount of red, green, and blue the user wants for an object's color, or a percentage of rotation from 0 to 360 degrees. Figure 2-6 illustrates how buttons and sliders might be designed for a graphical application.

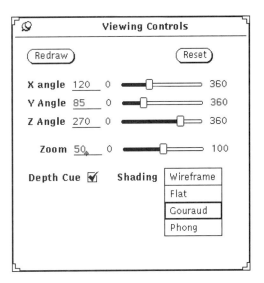

Figure 2-6   Examples of buttons and sliders.

The Application

An application is a software package designed to meet particular user requirements. For instance, a drafting program might provide graphical tools similar to those on a drafting table, and make it possible to create sophisticated layouts in less time than it takes to create them with traditional methods. In addition to providing the special advantages of computer technology, such as quick storage and retrieval and the ability to correct or modify existing material without "starting from scratch," such an application should be nearly as intuitive to the user as working with paper on a drafting board.

The application is the user's interface to the workstation's graphics capabilities. A good application interface is easy to use and provides intuitive access to the application's tools. Like the design of the window system, the design of graphical applications is based on a graphical user interface, and ideally, the window system's and graphics application's GUIs are one and the same.

Typically provided by independent software vendors (ISVs), application programs are designed to run on the graphics hardware produced by specific vendors. Chapter 1 briefly introduced several graphics applications, and Chapter 7 is devoted to the description of some of the most prevalent types of applications and their software needs.

The Application Developer

By the time the user receives the application software, it has been designed, developed, and debugged by computer graphics programmers who specialize in writing applications. To write applications, application developers learn what is most important to a particular type of user and then design a program that presents a logical work environment and provides the tools necessary to get the job done, enabling the user to work more efficiently.

Just as there are tools and interfaces for the end user, there are tools and interfaces for the application developer. These tools enable the developer to design application utilities, such as buttons and sliders, in an efficient manner. One of the application developer's most important tools is the **graphics library**.

The Graphics Library

The graphics library is the toolbox that the application developer uses to write application software for the user. Represented by an **application programmer's interface**, or **API**, the graphics library is a collection of software routines (computer code) that draw the geometric elements (called **primitives**) that are used to construct computer pictures. This resource relieves the developer of writing low-level code to create pictures; the routines in the library supply the primitives when they are called by a graphics program. To create a picture, for instance, the developer makes some design decisions, and writes code that references the routines in the graphics library. The graphics library makes application development more efficient because the developer does not have to tell the computer how to draw simple primitives and can concentrate on producing high quality software for the end user.

The graphics library works very closely with the computer hardware, which calculates the size and position of the graphical primitives. Once the library is implemented (programmed to run) on specific graphics hardware and is optimized to work as quickly as possible, it is ready for application development.

There are various types of graphics libraries. For instance, some graphics libraries can be used for programming two-dimensional graphics applications only, others are exclusively for three-dimensional graphics, and still others can be programmed for either 2-D or 3-D.

Some graphics libraries are designed to work with specific processing hardware. These are called **device-dependent** libraries. Some graphics libraries are **device-independent**, which means they can be implemented on hardware of various designs. Several **industry standard**, device-independent libraries have been approved by standards organizations. These are discussed in "Library Standards" in Chapter 8.

An advantage of any graphics library (as opposed to special purpose graphics software designed for limited use) is that features that are occasionally useful but would be too much trouble to implement or optimize for a single application can be justified when used for many applications. This is especially true about a graphics library provided by the system vendor, because the vendor can amortize the development costs over more applications than any large customer can. Another advantage of a graphics library provided by the system vendor (whether it is a vendor-developed library or a standard library that the vendor implemented) is that the vendor understands the nuances of the hardware and can use it most efficiently.

It is important to note that the graphics library has several levels of operation: the developer's level and the application level. First, the developer creates applications using the library tools. Once the application is developed, it is made available to end users. Because the finished application does not require all the tools that the developer needed to create it, it is provided to the user with a subset of the library. This subset, called the **run-time** library, enables the application (at "run time") to access the drawing routines that the developer included in the application package.

The Application Database

All of the information that must be accessed by the application while it is being used is called the **application database**. The application database stores all of the data that are used to control the application window, the calls to the routines that draw the picture primitives, and any other information required by the application to create pictures upon demand. Additionally, when the user is actively creating images with the application, some representation of the images and their attributes is stored in the application database until updates occur.

As an example, an electronic circuit designer might run an **electronic computer-aided design** (ECAD) application. The application database stores the data describing each circuit wire drawn by the designer. When it is time to make a change to the design, the circuit designer first requests that the application reproduce the original design. The application then accesses the design data from the application database, enabling the designer to modify the design and store the results back into the database.

Hardware and Software Interaction

This chapter has discussed a variety of graphics system components. Each of these must work interactively with the others as data are created by the user and the application, and as data are used by the processors and display device.

The graphics software and hardware have a symbiotic relationship. Conceptually, the process of producing a picture occurs as follows. The user communicates with the application software via the input hardware (such as the keyboard and mouse); this input is interpreted by the application and the graphics library, which use the hardware processors to make the mathematical calculations that compute the size, color, and orientation of the graphical picture and store the picture data to be drawn by the display monitor hardware. Figure 2-7 illustrates this process.

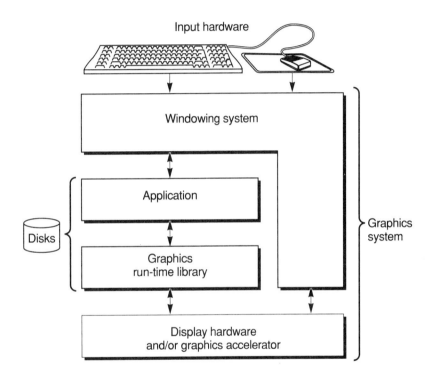

Figure 2-7   Flow of events between the graphics software and hardware.

In reality, many of these processes occur simultaneously, and describing the processing and display of a picture in linear terms is an oversimplification. The responsibility for many processes may be a joint effort of the software and hardware; how tasks are allocated depends upon the particular system setup. It is generally true that the more jobs and calculations (which may number in the millions during the display of a single picture) that can be accomplished by a specialized graphics accelerator, the faster the application will appear to run.

Peripheral Devices

This section briefly describes some of the special input and output devices for graphics, including printing devices, which may be added to the graphics system or work environment. "Output" includes both **soft-copy** output—from the graphics display and from video equipment—and **hard-copy** output from printers and plotters.

Button Boxes and Dial Boxes

In addition to the keyboard and mouse, some computer graphics systems may include one or more graphics function boxes, called **button boxes** and **dial boxes**. Like the keyboard's function keys, these devices can be programmed for use by a particular application. While button boxes provide additional programmable features similar to the keyboard's function keys, dial boxes can be programmed to issue events in a range, such as rotations from 0 to 360 degrees in three directions. The rotation occurs at the speed at which the user turns the particular rotation dial (in x, y, or z) and rotates in direct relation to the amount the user turns the dial. Figure 2-8 illustrates a button box and a dial box.

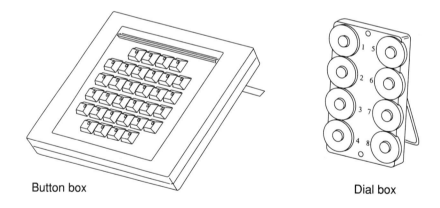

Button box   Dial box

Figure 2-8 A button box and a dial box.

The Graphics Tablet

The graphics tablet (or data tablet), used primarily in design environments, is a flat surface with internal electronic wiring, placed on a desktop near the graphics workstation. The surface of the tablet is often printed with a selection menu, specialized for the particular application. The data tablet can be used for creating designs or converting existing images into digital information for graphical display.

The user operates one of two input devices with the data tablet. The **puck**, a small device that behaves like a mouse (but is more precise), can be moved across the data tablet to indicate locations, to make design selections, or to indicate the parameters of an image to be digitized. As the user slides the puck on the tablet, the electronics within the tablet detect the motion and the system updates the pointer on the display accordingly. The **stylus**, which can be moved across the tablet like a pen on paper, functions similarly to the puck. To digitize an image, the user places a hard-copy image on the graphics tablet, moves the stylus or puck to selected points on the drawing, and transmits those points to the application by pressing down on the stylus or selecting one of the puck buttons. Figure 2-9 illustrates a data tablet with a stylus and puck.

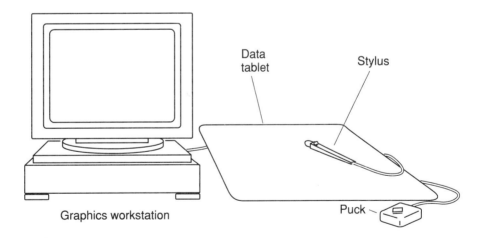

Figure 2-9   The graphics tablet, stylus, and puck.

Scanners

A scanner is another piece of electronic equipment designed to convert hard-copy images to digital information. Unlike a data tablet, however, the scanner does not require the manual drawing effort of a digitizing stylus. There are many types, but as an example, a photo scanner with a light beam is common for scanning documents. The scanner focuses the light beam on the image, and the amount of light reflected from the different parts of the document is measured by a photo cell. The resulting data are recorded in a file containing an electronic image of the document.

Video

New developments in multimedia technology make it possible to capture video signals for display on the graphics monitor. Video is making inroads into such applications as teleconferencing and image capture for desktop publishing.

A graphics system set up with video equipment can receive video input from a variety of conventional sources, such as VCRs, camcorders, video disc players, TV tuners, and video cameras. These images can be output to the graphics monitor, and in some cases, can be sent to different graphics workstations on the same **local area network** (LAN), an electronic networking arrangement covering a small geographical area. The video image may be continuous, or it may be output in a rapid series of still frames. Real-time video requires 30 to 35 frames per second.

For video images to be transferred to the graphics system, the images are converted by special hardware from analog to digital signal. They are then stored in memory and can be displayed.

Film

A film recorder sends graphical output to photographic film rather than to a graphical display. Instead of sweeping across the display screen, the electron beam sweeps across and exposes the film. Film recorders may have their own frame buffers, separate from the display device, or they may be mounted to the CRT. Film recorders can be used to produce high-quality images from the computer system.

Printers and Plotters

The **dot matrix printer** prints by firing tiny pins against an ink ribbon, pressing the ribbon against the paper. The paper advances one line at a time, and that line is printed. Color printing uses either one multicolored ribbon or a colored ribbon for each of the three colors to be mixed into composite colors. Rather than using red, green, and blue, as the computer display does, the color printer uses a CMY (cyan, magenta, and yellow) color model. Cyan, magenta, and yellow are the color **complements** (opposites) of red, green, and blue. As discussed earlier, light is additive and thus colors in the RGB model are mixed by addition; the addition of all RGB colors results in white. By contrast, printing is **subtractive**, meaning that colors are specified by what is removed, rather than added. The addition of all CMY colors results in black, and the desired color must be obtained by subtraction.

Because both the display output and dot matrix printer output use dot grids to define their images, graphical images must be **scan converted** by the graphics system to match the dot matrix output resolution.

The **laser printer** scans images from its own internal copy of the image data. The laser beam sweeps over the image and repeats the pattern on paper with printer toner. The laser printer generally prints a much higher quality image than the dot matrix printer, at resolutions of 300 dots per inch or more, and is therefore preferable for higher quality printing.

The **pen plotter** is a sophisticated printing device that has its own microprocessor for handling commands in a manner similar to the graphics library's drawing routines for graphic primitives. The microprocessor translates the drawing routines into incremental movements of the pen. The pen itself has exceptional movement capability. Pen plotters generally offer a precise printing method.

There are two types of pen plotters: the **flatbed plotter**, which contains a paper table and carriage that contains the pen; and the **drum plotter**, which stretches paper tight across a drum that can roll the paper forward and backward under a pen. Plotters are used in applications such as mechanical design and architectural design, where a high level of technical detail must be achieved. The **ink-jet plotter** produces hard-copy color images. The ink-jet plotter uses a dot grid to determine the location of an image. (As we discuss in Chapter 3, in "About the Raster," this is also how the graphics display functions.) The plotter's ink nozzle sweeps over the paper surface, spraying ink in the appropriate dot locations.

Graphics on the Network

Networked computing has made it possible for resources to be shared electronically among computers via client/server relationships. There are two client/server models: the **networked file system** model, and the **networked window system** model.

File System Networks

In the networked file system, multiple computer users on the same electronically-linked network can exchange data and share resources, such as software, disk space, and printing devices. Applications with intensive requirements can be handled by a **compute server**, while workstations and personal computers, acting as the **clients** of the server, make use of the server's resources and thereby optimize their own. Figure 2-10 illustrates a group of machines on a network.

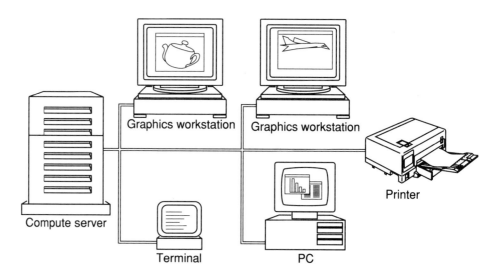

Figure 2-10 A networked system with a main server and multiple client machines.

This client/server arrangement is especially useful in workgroups where the same graphics applications are needed by many members of the group. The client machines can access data, memory, and application programs from the server simultaneously, just as if the resources existed on their own machines.

Window System Networks

In the networked window environment, the *client* is the *application* using the window system on a machine that can provide that application with the necessary resources, such as large memory and a powerful CPU. This client interacts with the window system server process. The server portion of the window system, which operates as a separate process, runs on a machine that provides it with the necessary graphical display and user interface hardware. For instance, the user might be running the window server on his or her graphics workstation, but can bring up a client application on a supercomputer residing elsewhere on the network. The results from the application are sent by the client on the supercomputer to the user's local window server. This window system model is a flexible one: the client and server may run on the same machine (and they often do). Figure 2-11 illustrates a networked window environment.

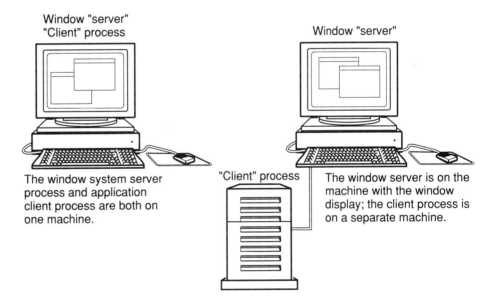

Window "server"
"Client" process

The window system server process and application client process are both on one machine.

"Client" process

Window "server"

The window server is on the machine with the window display; the client process is on a separate machine.

Figure 2-11 The networked window environment.

Conclusion

This chapter developed the terminology pertaining to the graphics system components, and the graphics application—the user's specialized graphics software package. Computer graphics is not a function of graphics software or hardware exclusively, but of the coordination of events between the many subsystems employed by each. Additionally, computer graphics requires hardware programmers, application developers, and users with special needs and ideas for how to represent complex notions visually.

Chapter 3 discusses the special properties of the **raster graphics** system and the specialized capabilities that make it possible to display complex graphical pictures.

Displaying Graphics

This chapter introduces the technology that makes it possible to produce complex color graphics images and display them on the graphics monitor. Topics include:

- Raster graphics

- Frame buffers

- Multi-bit systems

- Color graphics

Raster Technology

Because **raster graphics** enables us to create beautiful, realistic pictures, it is the most common computer graphics technology in use today. Raster technology makes it possible to simulate the effects of color, light, and shade on realistic objects, and to handle exceptionally minute picture detail. These effects are accomplished with a device called a display controller (or video controller) that reads a set of numbered arrays from the frame buffer display memory, and uses this information to scan images onto the display monitor. The frame buffer is so called because it temporarily stores or *buffers* a full frame of display information at a time. The frame buffer contains all of the pixel values (monochrome, gray scale, or color) that describe the picture to be displayed on the computer screen. These pixel values collectively comprise the **raster**.

The raster device essentially is a grid divided into many pixels. Each pixel can be treated individually, and thus very small portions of a picture can be modified without affecting the entire picture. This is an important innovation. Older technologies required the entire computer screen to be redrawn whenever even a small change was made. Raster graphics pictures can be extremely complex, and can require a great amount of compute power, thus the capability of making precise and efficient changes to a picture is a critical feature of this technology.

About the Raster

If you look closely at the black and white pictures in a newspaper you will notice that dark tones are created by printing many dark dots close together, and lighter tones are created with fewer dots printed farther apart. This method of producing images with dot patterns is called **halftoning**. Graphical **objects** are composed in a raster of tiny dots (pixels) in a manner somewhat similar to that of halftone images.

On a basic monochrome monitor, for example, the graphics system displays pictures by illuminating pixels in the pattern of the picture. Figure 3-1 illustrates the frame buffer and corresponding picture display on a simple monochrome monitor.

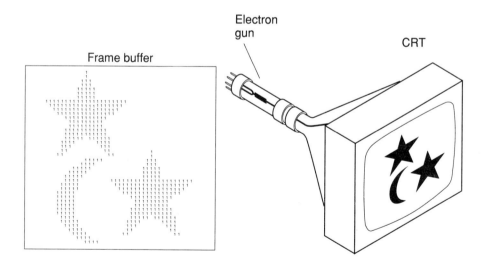

Figure 3-1   The electron beam writing a pattern of pixels to the raster display.

For simplicity, illuminated pixels are illustrated as darkened dots, whereas an actual pixel is typically black when it is off. Also, the pixels are greatly enlarged in proportion to the raster device. In reality, depending upon the size and resolution of the CRT, the display may contain more than a million pixels.

About the Frame Buffer

The frame buffer, the graphics system's display memory, contains the state of all the pixels on the raster at any given time. It supplies this information to the electron beam as it rapidly scans and refreshes the raster. When the picture changes (such as when an object is moved to a new location on the display area or is rotated into a new position), the frame buffer is updated, and the electron beam illuminates the pixels in the new picture pattern.

The display information for each of the pixels is stored in the frame buffer in computer **bits**—short for **binary digits**—which can be turned on and off. These are represented in the frame buffer as ones when on and zeroes when off. A monochrome display, the most simple raster device, has one bit for each pixel on the raster. It can display one of only two values at each pixel, such as black (off) and white (on). These two values might instead be black and green, or black and amber, which is why we use the term **monochrome** rather than **black and white**. Figure 3-2 illustrates the frame buffer bit values for a simple design on a monochrome raster display.

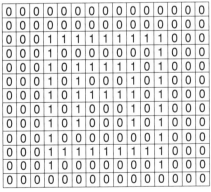

Frame buffer   Display on monitor

Figure 3-2   The frame buffer's relationship to the raster display.

The array of values in the frame buffer for a given picture is often called the **bitmap**, particularly for monochrome (single-bit) displays. Another useful term, **pixmap**, is used for the array of pixel values in the raster in more complex gray scale or color monitors, which have more than one bit for each pixel in the raster display. We will discuss multi-bit displays shortly.

Pixel Addresses and 2-D Space

Each pixel has a numbered address on the raster grid so that the pixel can be identified and then modified (for example, its color can be changed). To understand how pixels are addressed, think of a piece of graph paper. The graph lines are numbered along the bottom axis and up the left vertical axis of the page. Every intersection of lines on the graph paper can be identified by its corresponding numbers. The graph forms a **coordinate system**, and each address is a **coordinate point**.

The graphics display surface is similarly described by a coordinate system. The horizontal edge of the coordinate system is known as the **x-axis**, and the vertical edge is known as the **y-axis**. Each pixel address (in two-dimensional graphics), is identified by its number at the intersection of x and y: x is always the first number in the address, and y is always second. Figure 3-3 illustrates an enlarged portion of a raster grid, with pixel address 3, 4 selected.

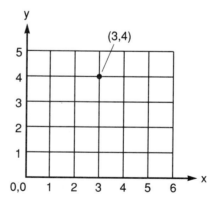

Figure 3-3   Pixel address 3, 4 selected on the raster.

Having identified a pixel address, the graphics system can illuminate the corresponding pixel. Figure 3-4 illustrates an illuminated pixel at address 3, 4. For the purpose of this discussion, we assume a convention that a pixel is the geometric unit above and to the right of the pixel address, although this is not a general rule. Note also that on many computers the raster grid is numbered beginning with the upper left corner (because that is where the scan line process begins at each refresh), but for simple convention, we refer to the lower left corner as the **origin** (0, 0)—the location where both x and y begin.

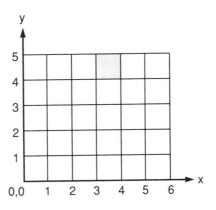

Figure 3-4   The illuminated pixel at address 3, 4.

Pixel Addresses and 3-D Space

Three-dimensional space is artificially created with geometry. A three-dimensional coordinate system, similar to the x-y coordinate system in 2-D, is mathematically defined as a space with height, width, and depth. The 3-D volume is represented by a third axis, called the **z-axis**. This defined space makes it possible to draw objects that not only appear to be three-dimensional, but that can be rotated in three dimensions to be viewed from many angles.

Selecting a coordinate point in 3-D is the same as in 2-D, except that three coordinates must be specified in the order x, y, z. For example, coordinate point (3, 5, 4) is three coordinate points along the x-axis, five coordinate points up the y-axis, and four coordinates inside the virtual 3-D space, along the z-axis. Figure 3-5 illustrates coordinate point (3, 5, 4).

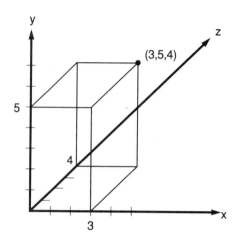

Figure 3-5   Coordinate point (3, 5, 4) in 3-D space.

We will discuss both two-dimensional and three-dimensional space in more detail in "Drawing in 2-D" and "Drawing in 3-D" in Chapter 4.

Multi-Bit Displays

Gray-scale and color monitors are equipped with multiple bits in the frame buffer for each pixel on the raster device. Because pictures are created with dots of color (or gray values) the complexity of the pictures that can be created with the graphics system is directly related to the variety of color or gray values the display is capable of producing. The number of colors the display can produce is dependent on the number of bits per pixel in the frame buffer. Graphics systems commonly have 8 or 24 bits per pixel, and highly sophisticated display devices may have over 100 bits for each pixel. This section first discusses color displays and then gray-scale displays.

True Color

There are two basic methods for producing color in computer graphics: **true color** and **pseudo color**. The method used depends on the amount of display memory contained in the frame buffer. True color (also called **RGB color**) provides unlimited freedom for combining colors from a large color palette composed of many more colors than the eye can distinguish. This method is called true color, because the range of colors in the real world are likewise too numerous, and the differences between similar color hues too subtle, to be individually distinguishable from one another. Although our eyes cannot detect subtle differences in color hues, without a great range of colors at our disposal, we cannot create truly realistic graphical pictures.

With true color, we specify some mix of red, green, and blue to create the desired color. This process is based on the RGB color model, introduced in "The Graphical Display" in Chapter 2. The color model is represented by an **RGB color cube**, illustrated in Figure 3-6. The cube has three dimensions, because the color space has three primaries; the color cube is a standard model that illustrates the six main color hues—red, green, blue, cyan, magenta, and yellow—plus black, white, and the gray scale, from which all other colors in the palette are combined.

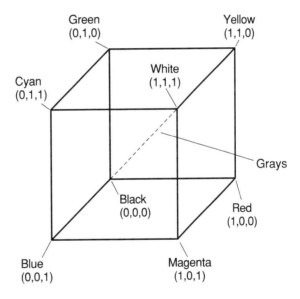

Figure 3-6   The RGB color cube.

The six main color hues are represented at the cube's vertices. Notice that each color is represented by an **RGB triple**—the amount of red, green, and blue in its makeup. We can mix an immense variety of colors in between each of these eight hues. To do this, we specify a color by its coordinates on the cube by selecting its RGB components between zero and 1. For instance, a pure orange hue could be obtained by specifying the RGB triple halfway between yellow and red. This would be (1, .5, 0), or a full red component, half a green component, and no blue. The range of aqua-blues lies between pure blue and cyan, the range of aqua-greens between cyan and green, the range of yellow-greens between the vertices of those hues, and so on. Notice also that any color, from its location on the color cube, can be mixed directly with white or with black. Mixing any color with white or black changes its brightness. As white is added, the color turns pastel; as black is added, the color becomes a darker value of that hue.

The user can access these color ranges through the graphical interface to an application. Typically, slider bars (see "The Application" in Chapter 2) for each of the primaries can be manipulated dynamically to create the full range of values. By using a mouse button and its pointer in the application window, the user can move each of the three sliders in a range from 0 to 255—256 values each for red, green, and blue. By moving the slider bars, the user selects an intensity level for the CRT's electron beam from among a great range of colors, and communicates this to the graphics system. The possible combinations of colors are $256 \times 256 \times 256$, which equals approximately 16.7 million color values.

Sample Color Systems

We have introduced the most elaborate color system to illustrate the full potential of color graphics displays. To display any color from a palette of 16.7 million colors requires a graphics display with 24 bits or more per pixel in its frame buffer. While many graphics applications require this level of display sophistication, others that must keep costs low typically use displays with smaller frame buffers. This section describes how colors are displayed when the graphics system cannot use the entire 16.7 million color palette.

As a simple example of a color system, consider a hypothetical frame buffer with 3 bits for each pixel. (In reality, systems are commonly 1-bit, 8-bit, or 24-bit, and other than the one-bit system, an odd number of bits is rare.) In a 3-bit system, one bit could be assigned to each of the three primaries: red, green, and blue. Because each bit can be turned on or off, there are two values for each bit. Color combinations are created with the three primaries by turning certain bits on and certain bits off. Mathematically, the number of colors that can be displayed at each pixel with the hypothetical 3-bit frame buffer is represented as follows: 2^3, or $2 \times 2 \times 2 = 8$. (The 2 represents the two values of each bit, and the 3 is the number of bits per pixel.) This means that there are eight possible color values at each pixel.

Figure 3-7 lists the color values that are possible with the 3-bit frame buffer. When all bits are on (1, 1, 1), the pixel is white; and when all bits are off (0, 0, 0), the pixel is black. Blue and green in the absence of red create cyan (aqua); blue and red in the absence of green create magenta; and red and green in the absence of blue create yellow. Note that the three colors obtained by mixing combinations of red, green, and blue are the opposites, or **complements** of the primary hues. Cyan is the complement of red; magenta is the complement of green; and yellow is the complement of blue. Combining a color with its complement results in gray or white. (Note also, that these are the same hues illustrated at the vertices of the RGB color cube.)

Composition in bits			Pixel color
Red	Green	Blue	
1	1	1	White
0	0	0	Black
1	0	0	Red
0	1	0	Green
0	0	1	Blue
0	1	1	Cyan
1	0	1	Magenta
1	1	0	Yellow

Figure 3-7 The color values that are possible with a 3-bit raster display.

A 3-bit frame buffer would obviously yield a limited range of displayable colors. With a greater number of bits per pixel, we have the capability of modifying a pixel's color or shade of gray on a more subtle level.

An increased number of pixel bits in the frame buffer means an exponential increase in the number of color values that can be displayed at each pixel. For example, if the graphics system had twice the memory—6 bits per pixel, instead of 3—it could display eight times as many color values: $2^6 = 2 \times 2 \times 2 \times 2 \times 2 \times 2 = 64$ displayable colors. Now 64 colors can be mixed from the primary hues (red, green, blue), plus their complement hues (cyan, magenta, and yellow), plus white and black. The eye can detect many more than 64 gradations in color, however, and a 6-bit frame buffer does not provide a color range suitable for realistic graphics. To illustrate pictures with complex color variations, the graphical display must be equipped with at least 8 bits per pixel, which makes it possible to display 2^8, or 256 colors.

Pseudo Color

Typically, systems with fewer than 24 bits per pixel display colors by indexing them in a color lookup table, or **color map**, which is a selection of colors chosen for the particular application. Instead of designating a specific RGB mix, index numbers in the color map are specified for any color displayed. This method, called **indexed color** or **pseudo color**, typically provides the application with 256 color selections. The term pseudo color comes from the fact that the eye can distinguish many more than the limited range of color values this system can display, and so the color map cannot accurately depict the true range of colors visible in our world.

Indexed color systems are not typically programmed to portray colors directly from their bit values, as this would greatly restrict the palette from which we could choose our colors. It would be like choosing colors from a box of crayons instead of from a full-spectrum rainbow. The color CRT is capable of displaying millions of colors, and we want to be able to choose from among them. To do this, we design the color map for the particular application, with a hand-picked subset of colors from the 16.7 million color palette. Figure 3-8 illustrates a portion of a sample color map.

Index	Red	Green	Blue	Result
0	0	0	0	Black
1	255	0	0	Pure Red
2	167	24	28	Rust Red
3	128	98	78	Brown
4	91	91	91	Light Gray
5	76	89	212	Royal Blue
6	0	0	255	Pure Blue
7	47	187	215	Sea Green
⋮	⋮	⋮	⋮	⋮
255	255	255	255	White

Figure 3-8   An abbreviated color map.

An Introduction to Computer Graphics Concepts

In the color map there are as many entries as there are pixel values, so there are 256 (0 to 255) color map entries for an 8-bit frame buffer. Each of the 256 possible bit combinations in the 8-bit frame buffer, rather than directly dictating the intensity of the electron beam, references an entry in the color map. Figure 3-9 illustrates the process by which colors from the color spectrum are selected for an application on an 8-bit system.

a. Colors are selected for the color map during application development.

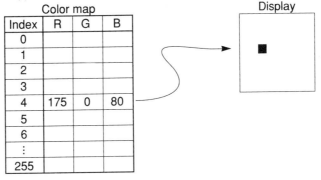

b. Application accesses the color map and writes color to the pixel.

Figure 3-9   An 8-bit pixel.

In this example, the application developer selected and assigned colors from the color palette to a 24-bit color map during application development. Each color map index entry makes use of 8 bits each for red, green, and blue. Thus, although the number of colors that the application can use is limited to 256, each of the colors can be selected from a range of subtle hues. At application run time, the 24-bit color map entries are accessed, and their values mapped to the 8-bit display.

When and by whom the color map entries are selected varies, but they are ideally under the control of the user. Perhaps the user is running a program that is capable of drawing realistic scenes, such as landscapes and seascapes. An autumn landscape in daylight might make use of a 256-entry color map in a range of greens, yellows, and oranges, whereas a seascape at sunset would be better suited to a color map with a selection of entries in blues and greens for water, and reds for the setting sun. If the color map had an equal spread of colors across the RGB color values, the user would not be able to access the more subtle values of a particular hue.

Gray Scale

Gray-scale display is a special case of color. Refer back to the color cube in Figure 3-6, and note that grays are represented by the dotted line between white and black. White is the result of combining whole values of the three primary colors, black is the absence of all color, and grays comprise the gamut in between. Obtaining any level of gray between black and white is a matter of mixing equal amounts of each of the three primaries.

One of the differences between gray-scale monitors and color monitors is that the pixel is singular, rather than a triad of red, green, and blue (see "The Graphical Display" in Chapter 2), and there is only one electron gun. Another difference is that increased freedom to choose from unlimited shades does not necessarily pay off. The cost of the graphics display increases with larger amounts of frame buffer display memory, and because we can distinguish differences in fewer grays than colors, 8 bits per pixel tends to be plenty for gray scale.

As with color, we can map the bit values to a color map (the gray-scale equivalent is a **gray ramp**) to select from a greater range of values than the direct bit values. Unlike color, the map contains one number per index entry, rather than three. This number is a composite of the red, green, and blue components, which are always equal.

An Introduction to Computer Graphics Concepts

Multi-Bit Frame Buffers

Because the raster screen is a rectangular plane composed of pixels, it is convenient to think of the corresponding bits in the frame buffer as **bit planes**. Multi-bit raster systems can be characterized by the number of bit planes contained in the frame buffer. Thus, a frame buffer with 8 bits for each pixel is considered to have 8 bit planes. The more bit planes, the more freedom a hardware programmer has to allocate these resources for various uses. Because there is a significant cost factor involved in adding extra hardware, the number of bit planes in the frame buffer depends upon the application's needs and the financial resources available to support them.

In a 24-bit system, if all 24 bit planes are dedicated to displaying the 16.7 million color gamut, the bit planes are divided evenly into 8 bit planes for each of the three primary colors: red, green, and blue. Figure 3-10 illustrates a raster and its 24-bit frame buffer.

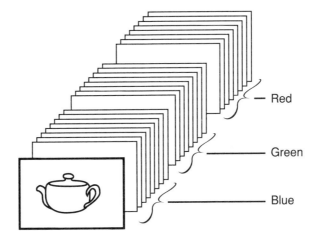

Figure 3-10 A raster device with a 24-bit frame buffer.

Double Buffering

Another way to allocate bit planes is to assign some portion of the planes to a second frame buffer. With two frame buffers, the graphics system can draw in one set of bit planes while displaying another set. This enables the graphics system to switch between two versions of the same picture and to update the picture out of the user's view, thus creating the illusion of smooth movement. To accomplish this, the programmer allocates some number of planes for one frame buffer (call this *Buffer A*) and an equal number of bit planes to a second frame buffer (call this *Buffer B*). For example, the bit planes in a 24-bit frame buffer could be divided into two 12-bit buffers. The result is a trade-off: there are fewer color choices (there are now 2^{12}, or 4096 colors, instead of 2^{24}, or 16.7 million colors) but animation is more realistic.

Double buffering occurs roughly as follows: as the graphics system is displaying the picture on Buffer A, the next stage in the object's transition is being drawn on Buffer B. When the contents of Buffer B are complete, the display is switched from Buffer A to Buffer B. Now Buffer B is displayed and drawing occurs in Buffer A. Figure 3-11 illustrates how the contents of the frame buffers are consecutively blocked from the display area as they are being drawn. Double buffering is especially useful for complex images where each change cannot be completed within one refresh cycle of the display.

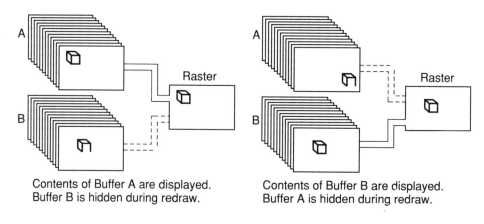

Figure 3-11   Switching from the display of Buffer A to the display of Buffer B.

Overlay Planes

Another method of allocating the use of bit planes is to allot some number as **overlay planes**. Overlay planes behave much like slide projector transparencies: they enable an image to be temporarily superimposed over another image (for example, one slide over another). In this manner, the data in the image beneath are not changed or **damaged** (affected) and do not need to be redrawn.

One method of handling overlay planes, illustrated in Figure 3-12, is similar to that of image planes. The application or window system can render (draw) into either one. A separate plane, called the overlay-enable plane, determines when the overlay planes are displayed. The display hardware tests the overlay enable plane for each pixel; when an enable plane bit is set to 1, the hardware displays the pixel from the overlay plane; when it is set to zero, the hardware displays the pixel from the image plane.

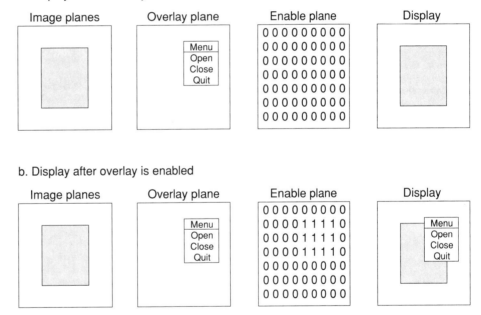

Figure 3-12 Overlay and image planes.

This method prevents damage from occurring in the graphics application window when menus or other windows eclipse some portion of the window beneath. The use of overlay planes is especially useful in applications that require a lot of time to generate the displayed image, as efficiency suffers greatly when the data must be regenerated.

Z-Buffer Planes

Z-buffering enables applications to determine the distance at which each portion of a picture lies from the viewer's eye point. This in turn enables the application to make the portions of an object visible that are nearer to the viewer and to hide the portions that should be concealed by other portions of the object. This process is described in more detail in "Hidden Surface Removal," in Chapter 4. Typically, 16 to 24 bit planes are allocated for Z-buffering.

Large Frame Buffers

Workstation vendors are developing high-performance graphics workstations with very sophisticated multi-bit frame buffers that provide a full spectrum of bit plane capabilities for graphics and windows, including double buffering, overlay planes, Z-buffering, and other window management planes.

Figure 3-13 illustrates a sample allocation of a 108-bit frame buffer. In this frame buffer, 48 bit planes have been allocated for image display, which means that the system can perform 24-bit double buffering. The display of certain planes takes precedence over that of others. This illustration shows the hierarchy, starting with the two cursor planes. These planes take precedence over others, because the mouse pointer (also known as a cursor) must be visible in the top-most window for the user to work in a window environment.

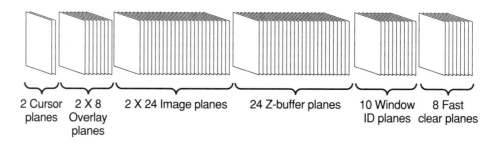

2 Cursor   2 X 8   2 X 24 Image planes   24 Z-buffer planes   10 Window   8 Fast
planes   Overlay   ID planes   clear planes
           planes

Figure 3-13 A 108-bit frame buffer.

In a windowing environment all windows have IDs (identification numbers) associated with them. These help the window system keep track of their order and location on the display. The window ID planes store the IDs for each pixel in the image planes currently being displayed. This enables the system to track double buffering, color map selection, overlay control, and other window operations.

The fast clear planes are used to clear the screen rapidly between frames. The illustrated frame buffer has eight fast clear planes, which enables the system to make use of four double-buffered pairs. With this method, one entire bit plane in the frame buffer can be cleared much more quickly (200 microseconds compared with approximately 10 milliseconds) than would be possible by writing every bit individually. When a picture is to be drawn on the raster display, the plane is cleared to 0, then each pixel that is written to the frame buffer also causes a 1 to be written into the fast clear plane at that same pixel position. When the display hardware draws the picture, each pixel with a 1 in the fast clear plane is displayed and each pixel with a 0 has the background color substituted. Thus, with each refresh, the background color is displayed for any pixels that do not contain image data.

Conclusion

This chapter introduced the terminology of the display hardware, and discussed methods of allocating bit planes in various system setups. As display memory increases, so do the special capabilities of the raster display system, particularly when increased display memory is coupled with increased hardware acceleration. Thus, the sophistication of the pictures we can create depends greatly on the sophistication of the computer graphics hardware.

Chapter 4 introduces the fundamental components of graphical pictures, and discusses how drawing in two-dimensional space differs from drawing in three-dimensional space.

Graphics Fundamentals

This chapter discusses the essential components of computer pictures, and introduces the concepts involved in drawing in two-dimensional and three-dimensional space. Topics include:

- Picture primitives

- Graphics in 2-D and in 3-D

- Picture quality

- Graphical text

Picture Primitives

At the basis of all computer-generated pictures is geometry. Because of the inherent geometry of the grid-based raster display, raster graphics pictures are composed of geometric elements, such as points, lines, circles, arcs, triangles and rectangles, also known as **primitives**. We essentially draw pictures on the raster by connecting dots—by drawing lines from pixel to pixel to create simple graphical primitives. These primitives serve as the basic building blocks in the construction of more complex objects.

In addition to these simple shapes, computer pictures often include more complex primitives, such as **polylines**, which are connected line segments, and **polymarkers**, which are small, two-dimensional shapes used to mark converging lines or other special locations on an object. Figure 4-1 illustrates several graphic primitives, a polyline, and a set of polymarkers.

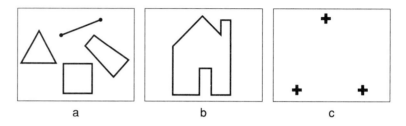

Figure 4-1   Graphic primitives (a), a polyline (b), and a set of polymarkers (c).

Dimension

We typically think of computer pictures as existing in two or three dimensions. The fundamental difference between 2-D and 3-D graphics is that two-dimensional pictures are flat, while three-dimensional pictures appear to have volume. Figure 4-2 illustrates two flat polygons in 2-D space, and two simple polygonal structures in 3-D space. For visual clarity, the lines at the front of the 3-D objects are thicker.

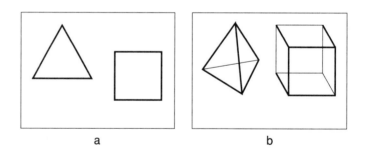

Figure 4-2   A 2-D triangle and square (a), and a 3-D pyramid and cube (b).

Note that the three-dimensional objects are created from two-dimensional primitives. Although these are very simple examples, they help to illustrate how 3-D objects are constructed: the user describes a surface shape, and the computer breaks it down into 2-D primitives. As an example, the user could describe a 3-D object for display that is as irregular as the shape of an oak tree, and the computer would divide the tree's surface into 2-D primitives. This is because the computer works with geometry. It calculates the shape, placement, and orientation of an object based on its geometric components, such as triangles and rectangles.

Note also that to illustrate the 3-D shapes in this book, we **simulated** three dimensions by drawing the semblance of 3-D objects on a 2-D surface. The objects actually are drawn on the same **plane** (for example, each page in this book is a planar surface when lying flat).

This phenomenon has two ramifications. First, the appearance of three dimensions can be simulated in two dimensions. Because it requires more memory to create three-dimensional pictures, and memory is expensive, one might want to *approximate* the appearance of 3-D using less memory. (Such a technique, discussed in the next section, is often used for cartoon animation.) Second, because the graphical display surface is flat, like a piece of paper, even objects that *are* 3-D must ultimately be reduced to 2-D for display on the CRT.

Simulating 3-D

As on paper, we can create the appearance of three dimensions on a graphics display by simulating a 3-D object's geometry with 2-D shapes. This effect, called **two-and-a-half-dimensions**, is sometimes used in graphics, usually for animation sequences. With two-and-a-half-dimensions, we can even create the appearance of a three-dimensional **scene** (an environment containing several related objects) by using various 2-D shapes to make it appear as though some objects are in front of other objects.

Figure 4-3 illustrates a two-and-a-half-dimensional scene that a user could create with a 2-D graphics application. The illustration contains several cylinders in different orientations. Note that the appearance of a 3-D cylinder turned halfway from the viewer is simulated with 2-D shapes. For example, the end of a 3-D cylinder looks like a flat circle when viewed from one end, but it looks more like an oval when the cylinder is turned partly away from view.

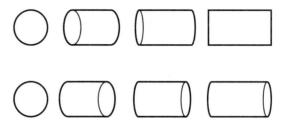

Figure 4-3   A two-and-a-half-dimensional scene.

These objects cannot truly be turned, or **rotated**, in 3-D space, because they are flat: the picture data are two-dimensional data that simply create the illusion of three dimensions. Thus, we are restricted to a frontal view of the scene and cannot take the same objects and look at the sides or the backs of them, and to create a new view of the scene, we must decide how to simulate the new orientation of 3-D objects with new 2-D shapes. Figure 4-4 illustrates a series of cylinders and the polygons required to simulate the appearance of 3-D.

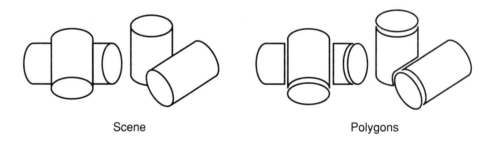

Scene   Polygons

Figure 4-4   The polygons required to simulate 3-D shapes with 2-D.

In addition to drawing 2-D shapes to create a 3-D appearance, the user must be able to simulate object **occlusion**—the effect of one object in 3-D space blocking another object from view. Because this requires intensive work on the part of the user, drawing two-and-a-half-dimensional pictures is used in special categories of applications such as animation sequences that are computed once in advance and then rapidly displayed in sequence. With this type of application, the speed of display, rather than the speed of creating the pictures, is the criteria for effectiveness.

Drawing in 2-D

The "Pixel Addresses" section in Chapter 3 discussed the two-dimensional drawing surface, which is described by two axes: an axis running horizontally, called the **x-axis**, and an axis running vertically, called the **y-axis**. These axes form a coordinate system that begins with an origin (0, 0). Each pixel has an address in the coordinate system, at an intersection of x and y. A pixel's coordinate point can be identified by its distance from the x and y axes.

Lines drawn on the raster grid are called **vectors**. To draw a vector, we can specify two endpoints and ask the computer to draw a line between them. Figure 4-5 illustrates vectors drawn from coordinate (2, 3) to (2, 8), and from (4, 5) to (9, 5).

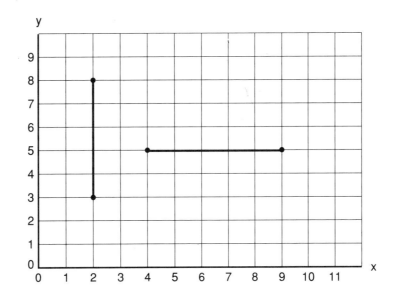

Figure 4-5   Vectors drawn from 2, 3 to 2, 8 and from 4, 5 to 9, 5.

Similarly, to draw a rectangle we can specify its four corners, or vertices. How the drawing application presents these options to the user is up to the application developer. As an example, the application interface might provide a tool for drawing rectangles. The user might select the tool with a click of a mouse button and then indicate the parameters of the rectangle by selecting a start point and dragging the pointer diagonally to an endpoint. Figure 4-6 illustrates how this might be done.

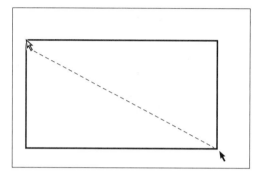

Figure 4-6   Drawing a rectangle with an application.

There are a number of ways that an application programmer might write the software code to draw the rectangle. Figure 4-7 illustrates a simple example of code that an application developer might write to create a rectangle and the final result on the raster. In reality, the vertices of the rectangle would be written as **variables**, and the actual numbers would depend on the points that the user selects.

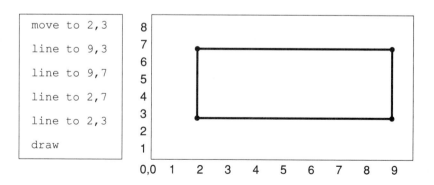

Figure 4-7   Code for rectangle: (2, 3) (9,3) (9,7) (2, 7).

An Introduction to Computer Graphics Concepts

Reducing 3-D to 2-D

In 3-D graphics, the computer calculates the 3-D geometry of objects. An image is described in **3-D space** in terms of its height, width, and depth. However, because the display surface is flat, the end result must be two-dimensional: a 3-D object must be reduced to two dimensions prior to display. This is part of a sequence of steps that occurs each time an object is displayed or manipulated in some way and then redisplayed. For instance, when the user rotates an object to a new orientation or scales it to a new size, the computer calculates the new locations and orientations of the picture's primitives in 3-D space and then translates this information into 2-D **screen space** and displays the picture on the screen. The process of reducing three dimensions to two dimensions for display is called **projection**. It is conceptually similar to the process of taking photographs of three-dimensional objects (people, for example) and reproducing the images on sheets of film. Projections are covered in Chapter 7.

Drawing in 3-D

Three-dimensional graphics is much more complex than 2-D for several reasons. First, the computer must perform more calculations in creating 3-D pictures. As we have seen, there is at least one extra step involved in drawing 3-D pictures, because they must ultimately be projected onto the two-dimensional display surface. Additionally, with 3-D graphics we have the freedom to draw in a voluminous space. Whereas in 2-D, a picture is a flat object displayed on a single plane, a 3-D picture can be many sided, and can move forward and backward in space.

To understand 3-D space, think of the x and y axes as forming a flat plane, like the end of a rectangular box. The z-axis is connected to this plane at one corner and runs perpendicular to the plane, representing the depth of the box. The three-dimensional space defined by these three axes, called the **view volume**, can be considered an infinite space in all directions. Figure 4-8 illustrates the viewer's **eye point** positioned along the z-axis.

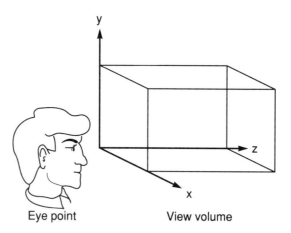

Eye point   View volume

Figure 4-8 The view volume: the 3-D space created by the x, y, and z-axes.

The Eye Point in 3-D Space

From the description above, the view volume might be considered a 3-D space that the user can see into, as if it were a room viewed from an open doorway. But in reality, the user can figuratively enter the room and view the images inside it from all sides. The 3-D graphics library enables the viewer's eye point to move around in the view volume and to look at any object from any angle.

This capability is sometimes described with an analogy to a camera (and is sometimes called the **synthetic camera**). Each view of the scene that is displayed on the CRT is like a snapshot taken from that angle. Imagine, for example, that you are walking around the outside of a stationery (unmoving) carousel. By the time you come full circle back to your starting point, you will have viewed the carousel from 360 degrees around its perimeter, even though the carousel never moved.

The graphics library supports this approach by using an additional coordinate system (very much like the x, y, z system) that can be oriented anywhere in the view volume. The synthetic camera's coordinate system, like the x, y, z coordinate system, is a mathematically defined space that creates the *illusion* of three dimensions. Because the graphics system knows the 3-D geometry of a scene, as if it existed in real-world space, the graphics system is able to produce images of the objects in the scene from all angles.

Figure 4-9 shows the eye point (or camera) focused on an image in 3-D space and the view that results when the eye point is placed in that location.

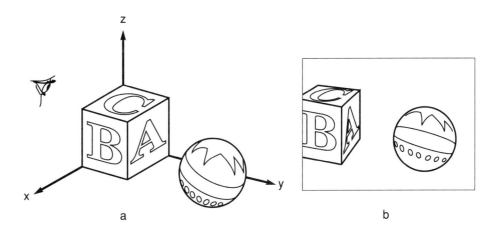

Figure 4-9   The eye point in 3-D space (a); what the user sees (b).

The advantage of this approach is that the objects in the scene can be calculated and placed once in the desired locations with respect to one another. The eye point can then travel around the scene.

Enhancing the Picture

In complex three-dimensional drawings—particularly those made of lines rather than solid surfaces—it is sometimes difficult to decipher the orientation of the object. Line drawings (called **wireframes**) tend to flatten out the dimension, and the lines closest to the viewer do not necessarily appear to be so. Additionally, artifacts such as a jagged appearance to the lines in an object can appear in graphical pictures. This section discusses methods that address these issues and clarify or improve the quality of raster graphics images.

Depth-Cueing

A complex image can be visually confusing, particularly a wireframe image in which all lines are visible front and back. For instance, a wireframe drawing of a building interior, with every floor, window, wall, and piece of furniture described by a line segment would be very difficult to decipher visually, and the user would not want to render the elements with solid surfaces, because it is important, in this case, that all elements be visible.

The **depth-cueing** technique helps to establish visual clarity by reducing the intensity of the image color in the portions of the image that are farther away from the viewer. This can be done on many levels so that there is a gradual fading of the image as it recedes from the eye point. Figure 4-10 illustrates a simple example of depth-cueing. Color Plate 2 shows an actual example of depth-cueing used in a design environment.

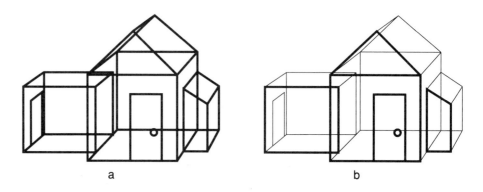

Figure 4-10 An image without depth-cueing (a) and with depth-cueing (b).

Hidden Surface Removal

In Chapter 3, the "Z-Buffer Planes" section introduced hidden surface removal, a method that ensures that front faces in an object or scene appear at the front by testing to determine which faces are closer to the viewer. Hidden surface removal (HSR) determines the depth of the faces in the scene. Instead of using the application database, however, hidden surface removal usually stores the depth data in specially designated memory, called the Z-buffer. The Z-buffer, or depth buffer, contains a certain number of bits in memory for each display pixel, in a manner similar to the frame buffer. However, whereas the frame buffer stores a pixel value for the *color* of the object, the Z-buffer stores a pixel value for the *distance* from the viewer's eye point that portion of the object lies. Figure 4-11 illustrates the hidden surface removal process.

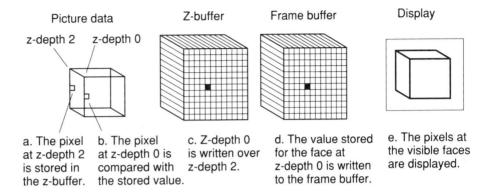

| Picture data | Z-buffer | Frame buffer | Display |

z-depth 2   z-depth 0

a. The pixel at z-depth 2 is stored in the z-buffer.

b. The pixel at z-depth 0 is compared with the stored value.

c. Z-depth 0 is written over z-depth 2.

d. The value stored for the face at z-depth 0 is written to the frame buffer.

e. The pixels at the visible faces are displayed.

Figure 4-11 Data in the Z-buffer.

This process tests to determine which faces are in front of other faces and removes those surfaces that should be hidden. First, the Z-buffer value at each pixel is set to infinity so that any value written to a pixel will be nearer to the viewer than the initial pixel value. As the application draws the object, the depth of the face at each pixel is compared with the depth of the last value written to the Z-buffer for that pixel. If the new face is closer, its color is written to the frame buffer, and the Z-buffer stores the new depth value, overwriting any previous value for that pixel. If the face is farther away, the face's pixel is discarded, and nothing is changed.

Hidden Line Removal

Hidden line removal (HLR) is a technique similar to hidden surface removal that is used to clarify the appearance of objects that do not have solid surfaces. With this kind of object, the viewer can see both the front and the back of the object simultaneously. HLR identifies and removes all lines that would not be visible to the eye point if the objects were solid, and results in a less ambiguous image. Note that like HSR, hidden line removal can make use of the Z-buffer if frame buffer memory allows.

Figure 4-12 illustrates three blocks that appear to be wireframes before hidden line removal, and solid blocks after hidden line removal.

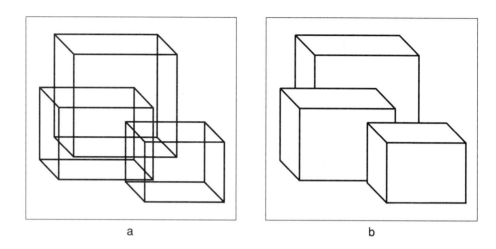

a   b

Figure 4-12   A scene before (a) and after (b) hidden line removed.

Aliasing

Drawing on the raster grid essentially involves connecting dots with lines. These lines must conform to the grid's geometry. With the exception of straight lines that run parallel with the x or y axes, almost all lines and curves cross the raster grid between pixels, rather than directly through them. Figure 4-13 illustrates an ideal line drawn from one pixel address to another. Because of the line's orientation, there is an ambiguity as to which pixels should form the line. This poses a problem, because the graphics system needs to know which pixels to illuminate.

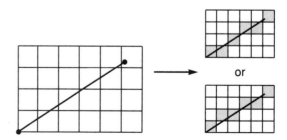

Figure 4-13   A line drawn between pixels.

To solve this problem, the graphics system must implement an **algorithm** (a set of defined steps) that determines which pixels are closest to the line being drawn. The raster examples to the right in Figure 4-13 show two possibilities for the final location of the line. With either choice, you can see that the end result is a jagged, "stair-stepped" line, rather than a smooth line. This artifact, or image irregularity, is called **aliasing**.

Every raster graphics picture is subject to the aliasing phenomenon. This is particularly true in the case of curves drawn on the raster screen, because a curved line, by nature, does not conform to a rectangular grid and must be approximated by a series of raster dots. Figure 4-14 illustrates an ideal curve on the raster grid and the illuminated pixels that form the aliased curve.

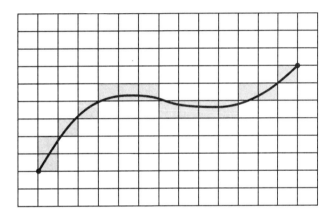

Figure 4-14 An aliased curve.

The degree to which aliasing occurs generally depends upon several factors. One is the resolution of the raster screen. With a high-resolution display or a very small monitor, it is difficult to see that the screen is composed of tiny dots. In a low-resolution display, the aliasing affect is essentially magnified, because the pixels are larger.

Another factor in the severity of the aliasing phenomenon is the **sampling** rate. In "Viewing in 2-D," Chapter 7 discusses how the last step involved in displaying pictures on the raster monitor is to **map**, or transfer the completed object to the pixels in screen space. This process involves using an algorithm that samples tiny points on the surface of the object to determine the relationship of each primitive to the rest of the object and to determine the object's final placement in pixels. If the sample points are too far apart, the final image will be aliased.

A third factor is the amount of data in the image. For accurate depiction of the image in pixels, there must be an appropriate number of sample points; more complex pictures require a higher number of sample points closer together to create a high-quality image.

Antialiasing

Methods for reducing the effects of aliasing are called **antialiasing** algorithms. Antialiasing algorithms take advantage of the multi-bit raster device's ability to display a range of colors or gray values at each pixel. If the pixels representing a vector are turned on to the brightest illumination and all neighboring pixels are turned off, the contrast is sharp, and so is the visible stair-step effect in the vector. Therefore, the basic idea behind antialiasing algorithms is that a vector will appear less jagged if the line is somewhat blurred. The solution is to vary the intensity of the pixels that are affected in the calculation of a line or curve. (Note that this cannot be done with a monochrome device in which the pixels are represented on a single bit plane in the frame buffer.) Figure 4-15 compares an aliased and antialiased line. The ideal line is drawn through the center of the pixels.

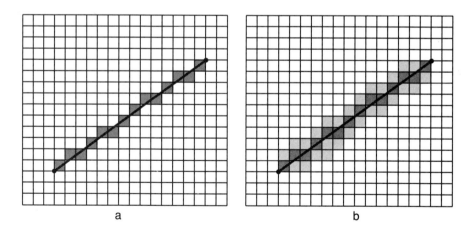

Figure 4-15 A vector aliased (a) and antialiased (b).

An Introduction to Computer Graphics Concepts

One way to vary the pixel intensity is to take an average of the highest and lowest adjacent intensity values and illuminate the aliased vector edges with those values, thus softening the contrast. More effective, however, are methods that use smaller and more numerous sample points to determine the object's placement in pixels. The intensity is varied based on the distance of the pixel sample point relative to the true center of the line, with the result that the pixels are brightest near the center of the line, and they are dimmer farther away. Note that increasing the frequency of sample points is considerably more expensive in computation time. For a comparison of aliased and antialiased objects, see Color Plates 3 and 4.

Graphical Text

It is important that we include some discussion of graphical text and how it is handled, because almost all graphics applications use text of some sort for annotating diagrams, labeling mechanical parts, naming separate viewports, and so on.

Representing text on a computer is an increasingly complex task. Early computer systems simplified the representation problem by restricting the characters to a limited set: enough for the English language plus a few special characters of common use, such as the dollar sign, the ampersand, and so on. These characters were standardized in the **ASCII** (American Standard Character Information Interchange) code set, which defines 127 characters. This proves to be inadequate for international use, where some Asian languages can require the representation of more than 50,000 characters. New codesets are currently being proposed to address the larger arena of the world's characters.

Codesets encode characters, but they do not describe how those characters should be presented visually. For instance, an ASCII code of 97 describes the character to be represented as a lower case *a*, but it does not describe the size, font or style to be used for that character. The task of describing the display properties of characters has traditionally been the job of the display device. Early display terminals greatly simplified the problem of character description by offering only one size, one font, and one style for the characters they displayed. Later, display terminals addressed this limitation by offering a small selection of sizes, fonts and styles for fixed-width characters. The disadvantage remained that characters could not be scaled to a different size or rotated to a new orientation. (See "Moving and Modifying Objects," in Chapter 7 for more information on scaling and rotation.)

Modern window systems combined with graphical display devices offer even greater flexibility by providing the tools to build systems in which characters are treated as graphical objects. Many raster systems store each text character in a bitmap (a rectangular block of pixels) with x and y coordinates, so that each character is like a miniature graphical picture. This allows multiple fonts in various sizes and styles to be combined, and to be rotated in a limited fashion. **Stroke fonts** (defined as vector strokes) can be scaled and rotated in the same manner as graphical primitives.

So specialized is the field of graphical text that special languages and display systems have been designed with the purpose of describing and rendering text in a flexible manner. A sophisticated set of capabilities is available with **PostScript**®, which is a high level device-independent page composition language with powerful 2-D graphics capabilities. The PostScript language defines text in terms of lines, curves, and solid-filled primitives, and performs **transformations**—changes in size and orientation—in a separate coordinate system so that the final placement of the characters on the bitmap is reserved until the last moment. (See "Viewing in 2-D," in Chapter 7.) Because of its power and flexibility, PostScript has become widely accepted as a de facto standard.

The discussion of text is a much larger topic than can be covered adequately in the context of this book. However, it is important to note that text is an important aspect of graphics packages, and the quality of text should be considered at the time of purchase.

Conclusion

This chapter introduced the fundamentals of drawing computer pictures in two-dimensional and three-dimensional space, as well as some techniques for improving picture quality. Computer-generated pictures are restricted in some ways by the geometric nature of the display device, but techniques such as antialiasing can be employed to outsmart these limitations and smooth the jagged edges that result from drawing on a pixel grid.

Chapter 5 introduces algorithms for creating computer pictures, including curve definition techniques that provide additional ways of smoothing out the visible geometry of computer-generated pictures.

Making Pictures

This chapter discusses the construction of graphical pictures using special algorithms that are well-known in the computer graphics community. Topics include:

- Application design

- Algorithms

- Graphical models

- Constructing graphical objects

Design Decisions

There are a number of ways to create computer pictures, depending upon the desired effect, the nature of the graphics library, the hardware support available, and the design of the application. An application developer, in designing drawing tools for the user, must make decisions about how those tools will create objects and what operations can be performed on objects once they have been constructed. For instance, the developer needs to have a sense of the amount of hardware support (acceleration) typically available for the application. Sophisticated pictures require extra time or extra compute power, or both; thus, the less elaborate the picture, the less expensive it is to create. Because the ultimate goal is to provide the user with affordable software that runs efficiently and provides all the necessary tools, the developer must consider the trade-offs throughout the design process.

Algorithms for Graphics

Many of the developer's decisions are based on established **algorithms**, sequences of steps or actions that are designed to achieve particular results. Algorithms provide methods for accomplishing tasks, such as creating curved surfaces, clarifying the appearance of objects, and applying lighting effects. For example, the developer might need to choose between a lighting algorithm that creates realistic results but is highly compute-intensive and one that creates suitably realistic results and takes less time. If the user is more concerned with speed than with realism, the less demanding algorithm is a more sensible choice. This chapter explores some of the many algorithms for drawing computer pictures and for rendering object surfaces with lighting and shading.

Graphical Models

A graphical model is an object that typically approximates an object of the real world with properties such as shape, size, orientation, and color. There are two general model types in 3-D graphics: the **wireframe** model and the **surface** model. The type of model chosen for an application depends upon the user's needs. For instance, the user might want simply to communicate a design idea, in which case a wireframe model would be appropriate. Figure 5-1 illustrates a teapot with a wireframe construction.

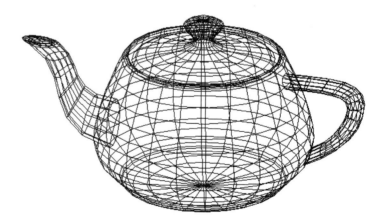

Figure 5-1   A 3-D wireframe model.

However, if the goal is to simulate a real-life object as realistically as possible, a surface model with complex colors, lighting, and shading is needed. (Note that a surface model is also known as a solid model, a term that can be confused with other technologies; thus the term surface model is used here for clarity.) Figure 5-2 illustrates the teapot constructed as a surface model with lighting.

Figure 5-2   A 3-D surface model with lighting.

There is an underlying geometry to both wireframe and surface models, because graphical objects are manipulated by their geometry—by the mathematical descriptions of the points, lines, and polygons with which they are made. The difference between wireframe and surface models is that the surface model can be made to appear opaque with solid color, light, and shade, thus concealing its underlying geometry.

The purpose of the model varies with the application. The teapot is a common model in computer graphics, because it presents interesting drawing problems for the graphics programmer, and it has varying surfaces for lighting and shading algorithms. In aerospace applications, the modeling object might be an airplane body or wing. The application might enable the scientist to simulate the effects of wind force on the plane. Molecular modeling applications simulate reactions among molecules through representational models, enabling the scientist to visually interpret events that cannot otherwise be visualized.

Constructing Objects

The distinction between wireframe and surface object constructions can become blurred, because there are ways to draw surface models that make them appear to be wireframes. Therefore, we need to clarify the terminology. A wireframe object is typically created from vectors—single line segments each connecting two coordinate points. Together, these vectors form the outline of the object surface. A wireframe can also be created from polylines—multiple vectors connecting a set of coordinate points. Surface models, by contrast, are constructed from polygons that create the surface, or "skin," of a closed space. The polygons themselves can be filled, making them opaque, or they can be hollow (with only boundary lines showing), leaving them transparent. Thus, a surface model may appear to be a wireframe. The object in Figure 5-3, for example, could have a wireframe (vector) or surface (polygonal) construction.

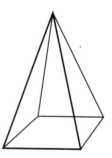

Figure 5-3 A 3-D pyramid that might be constructed of vectors or polygons.

Creating the Wireframe Model

The wireframe model of the pyramid requires eight vectors: one for each triangle edge and one for each edge of the base. To draw the model, the application needs to know how long the vectors are and where they join. We can describe this information in two concise lists to be stored in the application database. One list contains the model's **vertices** (endpoints where vectors meet) and another the model's **edges** (vectors). The vertex list describes the geometry of the model: where each corner is located in 3-D space. The edge list describes connectivity: how each vector is connected to other vectors at

An Introduction to Computer Graphics Concepts

their common vertices. When the user selects the model from a group of stored objects, the application draws the pyramid from the lists of edges and vertices.

In Figure 5-4, the table next to the pyramid lists three numbers (coordinates) at each **vertex**, or endpoint where vectors meet. These coordinates do not necessarily represent the actual placement of the object when the user sees it on the screen, but they provide the data from which the application can create the model when the user requests it. For simplicity, the sample coordinates for the object begin at the origin. Each base vertex is two coordinates (in some measurement system, not necessarily in pixels) away from its neighboring vertices on the base and three from the apex of the pyramid. The apex is one coordinate to the right on the x-axis, three coordinates up the y-axis, and one coordinate deep on the z-axis.

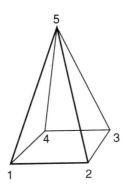

	a
	Vertex list

Vertex	x,y,z
1	0,0,0
2	2,0,0
3	2,0,2
4	0,0,2
5	1,3,1

	b	
	Edge list	

Edge	Vertex 1	Vertex 2
1	1	2
2	2	3
3	3	4
4	4	1
5	5	4
6	5	3
7	5	2
8	5	1

Figure 5-4   The vertex list (a) and edge list (b) associated with the pyramid.

Creating the Surface Model

To create a surface model for the same object, we need five polygons: four triangles and one rectangle. Instead of edges, the picture data consist of the **faces** of the model's polygons (also called **facets**). Each polygon face is defined by all of its vertices. To draw the surface model, the application needs to know how many faces the object has and where each face's vertices lie.

Figure 5-5 illustrates the pyramid with a number for each vertex and a letter (for clarity and convenience) at each face. The data for the model, to be stored in the application database, consist of a list of faces and the vertices for each.

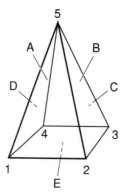

Face list	Vertices
A	1 2 5
B	2 3 5
C	3 4 5
D	1 4 5
E	1 2 3 4

Figure 5-5   The surface model and its face list.

Creating a Solid Surface

Each polygon face, or facet, can be filled with a color to make the model appear solid. Applications often provide the user with the option to generate images with hollow polygons or filled polygons, and to convert from one to the other at any time during the process. Because the hollow constructions can be drawn more quickly, the user can first create a model with hollow polygons, analyze it and fix defects or problems, and then convert it into filled polygons with added lighting for the final effect.

Problems can occur as the application draws the object from the stored data with solid-filled polygons. For instance, when the application enables the object to be drawn and viewed from various angles, the polygons at the back of the object can be drawn *after* those appearing at the front, distorting the object's appearance. Additionally, the application, unless instructed otherwise, will draw the entire object, including polygon faces that are not visible. In some cases, we might want to avoid the extra drawing time. This section introduces two common algorithms that address these problems.

An Introduction to Computer Graphics Concepts

Painter's Algorithm

The application developer needs to make sure that when the application reads the face list in the database, it will draw the polygon faces in the correct order so that the forward faces will be drawn last. In Figure 5-6, the pyramid is illustrated as it is meant to appear and as it might appear if the faces are drawn in the incorrect order.

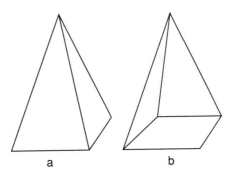

a   b

Figure 5-6   The intended appearance of the model (a); possible distortion (b).

The **painter's algorithm** ensures that faces are drawn in the correct order, from back to front. The faces are layered, as a painter might layer images on a canvas so that the final result is a scene that makes visual sense. The application accomplishes this by storing the depth order of each of the faces in the scene. When the application database provides the data for each of the faces, it gives their relative depth locations as well. The application then creates the scene with the forwardmost faces in front.

Back-Face Rejection

Figure 5-7 illustrates the pyramid as it should appear if the polygons are filled with a color (other than the background color). In this orientation, we see only two of the five polygons that make up the model. As a result, the three polygons that are not visible are unnecessary, and it might be inefficient to draw them. The **back-face rejection** algorithm eliminates the extra time required to draw portions of the object that are not visible. The data describing the hidden polygons remain in the application database, however, and, if the object is rotated so that the hidden portions come into view, the application will draw them.

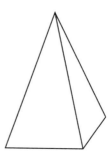

Figure 5-7   The surface model with filled polygons.

Efficiency Measures

Discussing the need for algorithm efficiency in the context of a simple structure such as the pyramid may seem odd. However, as models increase in sophistication, and as we begin to work with lighting and shading methods, the need for efficiency becomes more critical.

Data sets for objects can be immense, requiring storage and calculation of thousands—even hundreds of thousands of polygon faces—for a single object. The hardware must be able to compute the size and orientation for each polygon as well as its connectivity to other polygons and the color of each of the pixels representing the image. If the user wants to rotate the object, the hardware must recalculate the positions of each of the polygons in the entire data set and the new color at each affected pixel.

Figure 5-8 illustrates an automobile wheel rim composed of over 13,000 polygons. The time required to draw this object depends greatly upon the speed of the graphics system hardware and upon the method of drawing employed by the software. This section discusses several ways to reduce compute time.

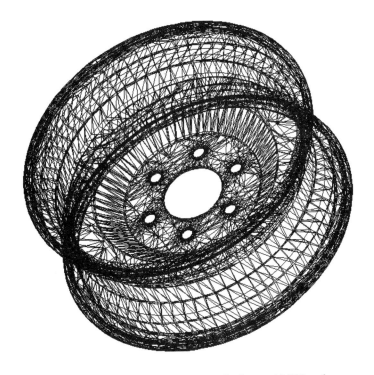

Figure 5-8   An automobile wheel rim composed of over 13,000 polygons.

Quads and Triangles

The polygons used in drawing graphical objects are usually three-sided (triangles) or four-sided (quadrilaterals), because these simple polygons are most efficiently calculated in hardware. If the polygons in an object are random shapes and sizes, with random numbers of sides, it is difficult for the application to compose a concise list of the model's faces to be stored in the application database. Additionally, if some polygons have three sides, and some have eight or ten, the hardware calculation of each polygon's orientation and connectivity will be belabored and drawing slow.

Some hardware systems are optimized for handling quadrilaterals (or "quads"), and some are optimized for handling triangles. A machine optimized to calculate quads can handle triangles by describing each triangle as a quad with one side of zero length. Similarly, a machine that is optimized to calculate triangles can handle quads by dividing each quadrilateral surface diagonally in half to form two triangles.

Figure 5-9 illustrates the division of a surface defined by quadrilaterals into a surface defined by triangles.

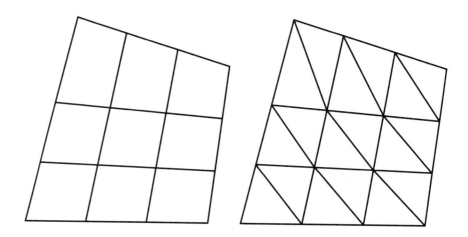

Figure 5-9   Quads divided into triangles for convenient calculation.

Tessellation

The process of subdividing a surface into smaller shapes is called **tessellation**. This process can be used in many ways in computer graphics, such as in creating special surface patterns. In this case, tessellation breaks down the surface of an object into manageable polygons. If the polygons describing an object surface have more than three or four sides, the software may tessellate the faces into the primitives that the hardware is optimized to handle.

Figure 5-10 illustrates a complex polygon tesselated into triangles.

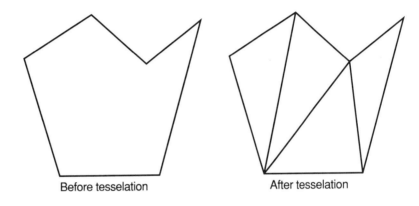

Before tesselation   After tesselation

Figure 5-10   A complex 2-D polygon tessellated into simple triangular primitives.

Quadrilateral Mesh

When the hardware is optimized for quads, the application usually composes object surfaces from a **quadrilateral mesh**. A quad mesh is a series of quads strung together. The special advantage of drawing in this fashion is that only the first quad in the mesh series needs to be defined by four vertex points. Each subsequent quad requires only two points to define its size and position relative to its predecessor, and the final quad in the series requires only one point. Figure 5-11 illustrates a quad mesh with a point indicating where the last quad in the series will be drawn.

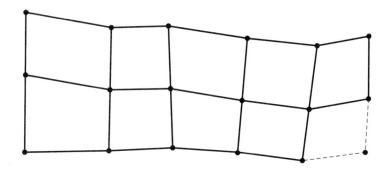

Figure 5-11 A quad mesh describing a portion of an object surface.

Triangle Strips

If the hardware is optimized for triangles, the application may compose an object surface with **triangle strips** in a manner similar to quad mesh constructions. With a triangle strip, however, three points describe the first primitive, and only one additional point is required to define each subsequent primitive. Quad mesh and triangle strip drawing methods eliminate the redundancy of drawing edges twice when they are shared by two primitives. Figure 5-12 illustrates a triangle strip.

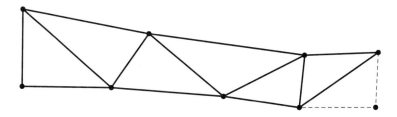

Figure 5-12 A triangle strip.

Triangles tend to be most efficient. One reason is that, as discussed earlier, each additional primitive in the strip requires only one additional point. This reduces the amount of data that the application database needs to store for any given object, resulting in fewer calculations for the hardware to handle.

An Introduction to Computer Graphics Concepts

Another advantage of triangle strips is that a triangle is guaranteed to be planar (flat): by definition, a triangle lies on a single plane. As a result, its orientation is predictable and is a simple matter for the computer to calculate.

Note that a plane is formed by any three points (for instance, in a triangle) that do not lie on the same straight line. Although a plane is considered infinite, stretching forever in all directions, it is usually illustrated as a quadrilateral that represents a section of the plane. Figure 5-13 illustrates a plane defined by three points.

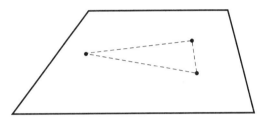

Figure 5-13 Three-point definition of a plane.

When a primitive has more than three points, there is no guarantee that it will lie on a flat plane. Thus, an object surface constructed of quadrilaterals may have polygons on its surface that are bent or twisted in space, and therefore pose difficulties for calculation and anomalies when rendering. Figure 5-14 illustrates several examples of non-planar quads, which are sometimes called "bow ties." Note that each of the polygon edges is straight but that the surface between them is twisted in space.

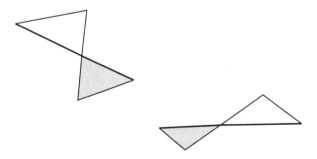

Figure 5-14 Non-planar quadrilaterals.

Curved Surfaces

To create a smooth, rounded object, such as the surface model of the teapot in Figure 5-2 or the rounded surfaces of a car body, we need a new set of algorithms for drawing smooth curves and for reducing curves to simpler primitives.

Because graphical pictures are ultimately displayed on the two-dimensional raster grid, curved surfaces present special problems. The application still must draw from point to point on the grid, and thus we are restricted to *approximating* curves with straight lines. The shorter the line segments that make up a curve, the smoother the curve will appear. However, to dictate to the graphics system each tiny point along a curve where we want the line to bend this way or that would take an inordinately long period of time.

Curve algorithms automate the process of calculating the sweep of a curve and the points along the curve where the line bends. The user typically provides the application with a set of data points that roughly describe the curve outline, and the hardware calculates the position of each segment of a polyline that approximates the curve. (This is sometimes called **curve fitting**.) A **high-order** curve is one that involves a high number of calculations to approximate a curve and thus requires considerable compute power; a **low-order** curve is one that involves fewer curve-approximating calculations and is therefore less computationally intensive.

This section discusses 2-D curve algorithms and then moves on to discuss how 2-D curve technology is extended to three-dimensional surfaces.

Bezier Curves

One of the most well-known curve algorithms, the **Bezier** algorithm, was originated by Pierre de Casteljau and separately by Pierre Bezier. The algorithm was initially created for the purpose of designing smoothly curved car bodies for a French car manufacturer.

To create a Bezier curve, the application requires user-defined endpoints—two that indicate the locations of the curve's ends and two or more **control points** in between. The control points serve as positioners for the shape of the curve: as the application creates the curve, the curve shape sweeps near the user-defined points. This is an iterative process. The algorithm searches for the midpoints between each of the selected control points and places new points at those locations. It then finds the midpoints between the new control points and places control points in those locations and finds the midpoints between them. After some number of these iterations, usually when each polyline segment is about the length of a pixel, the curve is drawn smoothly across the points between the curve ends. Figure 5-15 illustrates three iterations and the final curve.

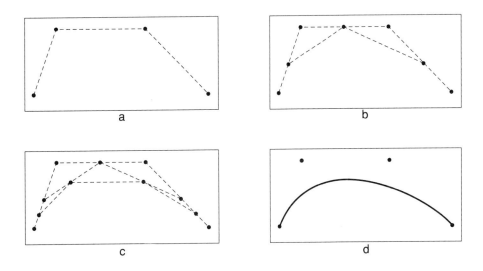

Figure 5-15 First (a), second (b), and third order (c) control points, and the final Bezier curve (d).

The advantage to the Bezier method is that it creates beautifully smooth curves. The disadvantage, for some applications, is that desired irregularities in the curve will be smoothed out. Additionally, because the Bezier curve is designed to flow smoothly between endpoints, precise Bezier curve control can require a large number of control points, which in turn require high-order curves that are computationally expensive. When it is important to exert local control on a more complex curve, the **B-spline** curve is the better option.

B-Splines

A **B-spline** is a sequence of smoothly connected curves, and, like the Bezier curve, it is defined in terms of control points. The application can model fairly complex shapes using a large number of low-order B-splines, which are easier to process than a set of high-order curves that produce the same shape. Another feature of the B-spline is that the curve shape can be controlled locally: a control point can be moved individually to a new location, affecting the shape of the curve surrounding it but leaving the rest of the spline intact. Figure 5-16 illustrates a spline curve before and after a control point has been moved to modify the curve's shape.

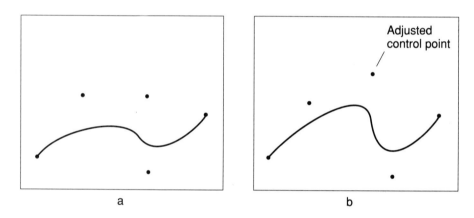

Figure 5-16 A B-spline curve before (a) and after (b) relocation of a control point.

NURBS

Newer B-spline technology has brought about the development of Non-Uniform Rational B-Splines (**NURBS**), which are especially useful in computer-aided design and scientific visualization applications due to their precision. A NURB is a complex curve that can be represented by a series of piecewise curve segments. This process is done with a sequence of **knots**, which are values that join the separate splines in a curve, each knot interval representing one curve segment.

An Introduction to Computer Graphics Concepts

NURBS have higher precision and flexibility due to the use of the knot sequence. Their relative spacing has an impact on the curve shape, and because the knots can be non-uniformly spaced, the user can exert extra control over the shape of the curve. This control can be local and does not need to affect curve segments in other regions. NURBS can exactly represent **conic** shapes, such as circles. A relatively small amount of memory is required to represent NURBS, making them an efficient curve definition method.

NURBS offer another feature over the algorithms discussed so far: we can apply a **weight**—sort of like a magnet—to each control point so that some control points have a stronger pull than others. More weight pulls the curve closer to that control point. Figure 5-17 illustrates the effect of one control point being given an increased weight.

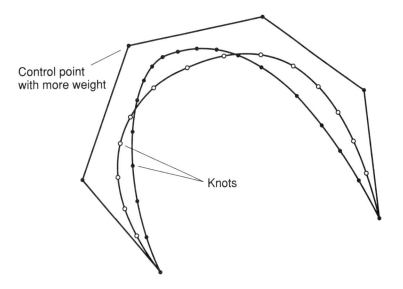

Figure 5-17 A NURB curve with evenly distributed weight (hollow knots) and with increased weight in one control point (solid knots).

From 2-D Curves to 3-D Surfaces

There are several methods for extending curve technology from the definition of 2-D curves to the construction of 3-D surfaces. This section discusses Bezier surfaces as an example, though surfaces can be constructed similarly with B-splines or NURBS.

With any curved surface method, the closeness of the approximation to the intended curve depends in part upon the precision of the control points and their distance from one another. This is because the final shape is still described by polylines or polygons that approximate a surface. The smaller the line segments or polygons, the more disguised the underlying polygonal structure will be in an object surface filled with color. The trade-off is that if tiny line segments or polygons are used to construct the object surface, more are required: this translates directly to more calculations for the computer.

The goal is to create a rounded surface with geometry, as efficiently as possible, and, ultimately, to achieve the appearance of a smoothly curved object when it is rendered with color and light. This section discusses several ways to produce smoothly rounded object surfaces.

Bezier Patches

Bezier curves can be used to create a smoothly curved **patch** surface, formed like a patchwork quilt. A Bezier patch is a quadrilateral mesh defined by two Bezier curves running in perpendicular directions (x and y, for example). The result is a patch that has four curved sides. For example, one patch might form a portion of the surface of a vase. Figure 5-18 illustrates the Bezier patch that will form a portion of the vase's surface.

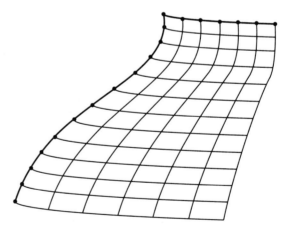

Figure 5-18 Two Bezier curves defining a patch.

To create the patch, the application computes the shape from user-selected control points to form one Bezier curve along the lip of the vase and then a second set of control points to form another Bezier curve along the vase's profile. The application **interpolates** the surface between the curves, which run perpendicular to one another. This means that the curve sweeps between the curve parameters, and all the intermediate values between the two curves are computed smoothly over the patch.

The separately drawn Bezier patches must be pieced together to form the final object. The polygons at the patch edges, called **control polygons**, must meet without gaps on the object surface. To accomplish this, the application passes to the application database a list of the edges and vertices along the mutual boundaries between patches. Figure 5-19 illustrates a portion of the intended vase, covered with three Bezier patches.

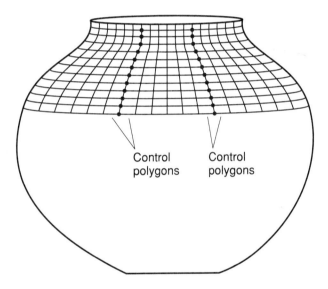

Figure 5-19 Three Bezier patches pieced together on a portion of a surface.

Surfaces of Revolution

Another technique for producing smoothly curved surfaces employs a rotation of data points about an axis to produce an object in three dimensions. This method creates a **rotational sweep**, also called a **surface of revolution**, which is a useful and expedient technique for many applications. First the user defines a set of 2-D points that describe an object profile. Next, the application sweeps them around an axis to create the three-dimensional surface. Simple examples of surfaces that can be created in this manner are the symmetrical cylinder and sphere. To create the cylinder, the user could place a straight line of data points parallel to, but at some distance from, the axis about which the surface will revolve. The data points for the cylinder are illustrated in Figure 5-20.

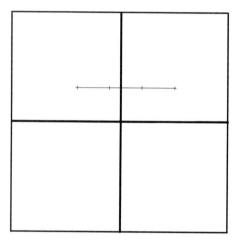

Figure 5-20 Two-dimensional data points for a cylinder.

As the application creates the surface of revolution it creates new data points in a regular sequence in 3-D space. Figure 5-21 illustrates the completed surface of revolution, as well as the cylinder rotated in 3-D space for a better view of its dimensions.

An Introduction to Computer Graphics Concepts

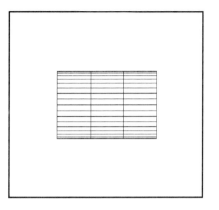 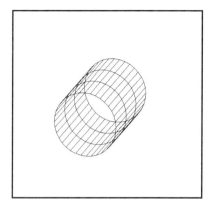

Figure 5-21 The cylinder created as a surface of revolution, and the cylinder rotated to a new view in three-dimensional space.

More elaborate structures can be defined in the same manner. Figure 5-22 illustrates the data points for a stemmed vase.

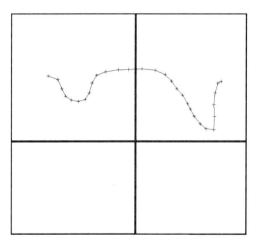

Figure 5-22 Two-dimensional data points for a vase.

Figure 5-23 illustrates the vase created as a surface of revolution, as well as a rotated view that illustrates its third dimension.

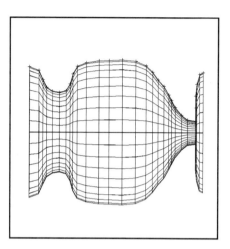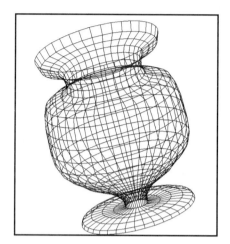

Figure 5-23 A three-dimensional vase as a surface of revolution, and the completed vase rotated to a new view in three-dimensional space.

Conclusion

This chapter introduced two types of objects—the wireframe object and the surface object—and discussed several algorithms that make it possible to create them. The type of model or object needed depends completely upon the application and the goals of the user, and many applications use both with regularity. The algorithms discussed so far present a highly flexible set of techniques that can be used to create objects and scenes of any complexity, depending upon the sophistication of the graphics library, the application software, and the supporting hardware.

Chapter 6 takes the discussion into the realm of graphical realism, introducing surface qualities such as lighting and shading, and techniques for creating entire, realistic scenes.

An Introduction to Computer Graphics Concepts

Surface Rendering and Realism

This chapter discusses the treatment of object surfaces and techniques for creating realistic graphical effects to simulate complex real-life environments. Topics include:

- Lighting models

- Ray tracing

- Radiosity

- Virtual reality

Lighting and Shading

In most real-world environments, several light sources affect the appearance of objects in that environment. **Lighting models** seek to reproduce these effects for realism. A lighting model is a mathematical formula that approximates the effect of light sources interacting with solid objects. The lighting model computes the color at a point on a surface, using one or more **light source** descriptions and the object's position, orientation, and surface type. Strong light focused directly at a portion of a highly reflective surface, for instance, is usually white or a very pale value of the object color.

Lighting models typically use several light source descriptions. Surrounding light, which has no direct source, is called **ambient light**. An environment in daylight, with no direct light, contains ambient light spreading uniformly in all directions. Ambient light is especially important in the use of shading techniques. Without ambient light, any polygons on an object that were not struck by a light source would be completely black, rather than a darker shade of the object's color.

Directional light comes from a particular source, such as the sun or an incandescent light bulb. This type of light shines on the surfaces of objects in the environment, interacting with those surfaces in three ways. Some of the light is absorbed by the surface, some is reflected from the surface, and some may be transmitted to the surface interior (refracted through the object) if the object is not entirely opaque.

Semishiny objects have **diffuse reflectance** properties. Much of the light striking the surface is absorbed, and thus the reflections or highlights from the object are diffused. Shiny surfaces, such as metallic objects, have low light absorption and high reflectance. The exceptional reflectance of a very shiny object creates **specular highlights**, which are bright highlights from small surface areas.

To compute lighting on an object, the application needs the orientation of the object's faces in space. Orientation can be determined by **normal vectors**, which are invisible vectors running perpendicular to points on a surface. Figure 6-1 illustrates examples of normals to various surface types.

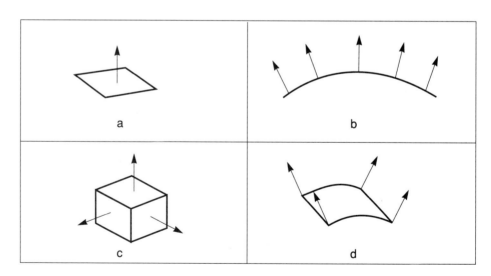

Figure 6-1   A facet normal (a); normals to a curved surface in cross-section (b); normals to cube faces (c); and vertex normals (d).

An Introduction to Computer Graphics Concepts

A **vertex normal** is calculated as the vector perpendicular to the surface at the precise point of the vertex. A **facet normal** (the normal to a planar facet) is either an average of the polygon's vertex normals, or the vector calculated to be perpendicular to the plane of the polygon. A non-planar surface, such as a Bezier patch, is a special problem because the normals change continuously over the patch surface. The number of normals used in determining the light on a face varies with the complexity of the shading method, and each of the three shading methods discussed in this section applies the lighting model to an object surface differently.

Flat Shading

The **flat shading** method, also called **constant shading**, applies the lighting model only to one point on each face. Each face is then rendered in a single color value that represents the amount of light interacting with that face. The result is a surface with a **faceted** appearance and a visible underlying geometry. Figure 6-2 illustrates a flat-shaded goblet.

Figure 6-2   A goblet rendered with a flat shading algorithm.

Smooth Shading

A more realistic effect can be achieved if the shading on the object's faces is not uniform. In real life, shading varies over the face of any surface, and smooth shading algorithms seek to simulate this effect. Instead of calculating the light at one point on each face, smooth shading algorithms calculate the light at multiple points and then smoothly blend the colors to incorporate the shading change across each face.

Gouraud Shading

Gouraud shading, one of the most popular smooth shading algorithms, is named after its French originator, Henri Gouraud. (Gouraud rhymes with Thoreau.) In Gouraud shading, the lighting model is applied at each of the vertices of each polygon face. The resulting colors at the vertices are interpolated across that face, which means that intermediate colors in the range between opposite vertices are inserted to create a smooth flow of color across that face. The result of the interpolation across the faces of the entire object is a smooth appearance, with the colors of lights and highlights blending across the surface.

Color Plate 5 illustrates an example of Gouraud shading.

Phong Shading

Phong shading, a more sophisticated smooth shading method, was originated by Phong Bui-tuong. The Phong shading algorithm is best known for its ability to render precise, realistic specular highlights. Phong shading achieves excellent realism by calculating the amount of light on the object at tiny points across the entire surface instead of at the vertices of the polygons. Each pixel representing the image is given its own color based on the lighting model applied at that point. Figure 6-3 illustrates a series of sample data points across the surface of a polygon.

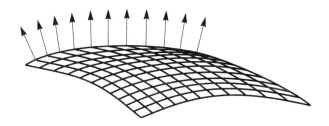

Figure 6-3   Data points for light sampling along the edge of one face.

Phong shading requires much more computation for the hardware than Gouraud shading and requires more expensive hardware that is optimized for this kind of rendering. However, Phong shading results in a much more accurate calculation of specular reflections, and is often worth the cost for applications that require highly realistic pictures. For an example of Phong shading, see Color Plate 6.

Multiple Light Sources

In real-life environments, a number of light sources generally affect the appearance of objects. Although it is much more computationally intensive to compute additional light sources, if there is adequate hardware support, doing so is an excellent way to increase the appearance of realism. Color Plate 7 demonstrates the use of multiple lights.

Visual Realism in Graphics

The pursuit of visual realism is one that requires a high level of technical achievement on the part of the graphics system and the application developer. Techniques for creating visual realism are mathematically complex, and the data sets are very large, making the design and manipulation of realistic pictures both challenging and time consuming.

It may not be intuitively apparent that it is an immensely difficult task to simulate reality with geometry and a computer. Real-world environments are highly complex, yet the nuances of light, reflection, shadow, and natural movement are intricacies that we tend to take for granted. In computer graphics, these intricacies must be described with geometric primitives and manipulated mathematically. Most of us are never asked to describe the geometry of clouds or to trace the directions light rays travel from numerous light sources as they are refracted through glass. Simply taking an inventory of the number of surface textures in a given environment, at a given moment, provides us with some insight into the challenges involved in the pursuit of visual realism in computer graphics.

The techniques used depend upon the application. Some applications require graphical realism and thus need software that makes it possible to create exceptional likenesses to real-life objects in addition to a high degree of hardware processing support. Some applications require speed and efficiency over and above heightened graphical realism. In other cases, the application may need realistic graphics *and* speed. The latter constitute the highest level of graphics sophistication and require exceptionally fast hardware. This section undertakes to describe a few of the major topics in visual realism and to present some of the applications for the techniques. Chapter 10 covers various application fields in more detail.

Real-Time Graphics

What is "real time?" One of the goals of visual realism in computer graphics is to make the calculations of rotations and translations appear transparent (undetectable) to the user. The image should appear to move freely in space, without distracting flickers or artifacts, at a speed that appears realistic, creating the illusion of direct manipulation of the objects in the image scene.

Applications such as flight simulators for pilot training benefit greatly from realistic movement: the more dynamically realistic and true to life the environment, the more the pilot is likely to gain from the experience. In this application, an entire simulated world must be maneuvered interactively.

Real-time graphics movement is achieved primarily through fast hardware processing and fine-tuning the graphics software to the hardware. (The hardware must be able to draw 30 frames per second or more.) In some applications, real-time movement is achieved with special animation techniques. For instance, one technique enables the application to bypass time-consuming steps in the animation process by precomputing the picture data and storing the animation sequence in progressive picture frames. With this method, pictures can be passed rapidly to the computer screen to obtain the effect of continuous movement, much like the rapid display of the many still images that make up a movie film.

Transparency

Transparency is useful in two environments: when the user would like to create an exceptionally realistic effect with translucent material such as glass, ice, or water, and when the user would like to view the inside of a volume without the obstruction of its external surface.

Realism with translucency can be created by tracing light rays as they refract through the translucent surface. These rays have a predictable pattern of bending as they refract and can be reproduced in a computer image.

Volume rendering techniques can be used to create solid volumes for visualization applications such as medical imaging. Such an application tends to be less concerned with lighting models and the interaction of light with the object than with eliminating surface obstruction, such as skin, to view the internal aspects of the volume. Software developed for this type of application might enable the user to produce a solid volume that can be converted readily from a solid surface to a transparent surface. ("Volume Rendering," in Chapter 9, discusses this technique in more detail.)

Ray Tracing

Basic lighting models depict the effects of one or more light sources as they strike an object, and in some cases (for instance, the Phong algorithm) produce realistic effects with highlights. Ray-tracing algorithms achieve a greater realism by calculating the paths of light rays from sources through the entire scene, including refraction through transparent surfaces, such as glass and water, and specular reflection from shiny surfaces.

Following the paths of the light rays is accomplished by testing each pixel to determine what the eye can see through that point. The eye sees light as it is represented by a pixel, having arrived there from some point in the scene where light interacted with an object. The type of object intersected by a light ray determines where that ray travels, whether it is refracted (bent through a translucent surface) or reflected (bounced off an opaque surface), and how widely it is scattered.

Light rays can be traced from the light source to the eye point, which is called **forward ray tracing**, or from the eye point back to the light source, which is called **reverse ray tracing**. Because reverse ray tracing takes into account only the rays that can actually be seen by the viewer's eye (as opposed to every light ray scattering in every direction from every source), the latter method is more efficient and more practical. Figure 6-4 illustrates a ray traced from the eye point to the object, and back to the light source.

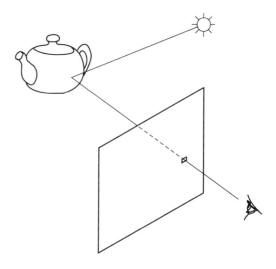

Figure 6-4   The eye point viewing an object model in a scene subject to a light ray.

The reverse ray-tracing algorithm tests each ray that can be viewed by the eye point to determine which objects in the scene have been intersected by the ray and which light components (diffuse or specular) are present. The type of light components to be computed depend on the object's surface type—whether it is opaque or translucent, shiny or non-reflective. The algorithm also determines the intensity of the light at that location. Once these tests are performed, the color that results from the combination of each of these factors can be determined for the representative pixel.

The algorithm is applied to each pixel, and the result is an accurate computation of the color that is viewed at every point on the display. A diffuse reflection from an opaque red object, for instance, may appear pink because of the interaction of white light with the surface color; however, a more intense specular reflection from the red surface may appear white because the intensity of the light ray dominates.

At the time of this writing, developments in ray tracing technology are leading toward more efficient methods of calculating light and reflection in complex lighting environments, but even with the short cuts provided by the reverse ray tracing method, it is still a very computationally-intensive technique. Ray tracing creates highly realistic scenes, but real time movement of ray traced images is possible on very simple scenes only. This is partly because ray tracing is **view-dependent**. As described above, light rays are traced between the light source and the viewer's eye point, or vice versa. This means that a change as minute as a slight shift in the position of the eye point would require a recalculation of the entire scene. Thus, in lieu of faster computers, a view-independent rendering algorithm is required for real time viewpoint movement.

Color Plate 8 illustrates a ray-traced scene with specular reflections as well as refractions through transparent objects.

Radiosity

Just as ray tracing is a sophisticated and accurate method of calculating complex lighting effects in a reflective environment, radiosity is a similarly sophisticated and accurate method of calculating lighting in a diffuse lighting environment.

Rather than tracing light rays, radiosity algorithms compute the effects of light energy in lighting environments. As in real life, this energy comes not only from light sources but from other surfaces that are affected by the same light source. For instance, if a blue light shines on a white wall, the wall reflects a certain amount of this blue light onto other surfaces in the room.

For radiosity, all of the surfaces in the environment are broken down into tiny patches, each of which interacts with all of the patches in the rest of the environment. Each surface is treated as an **emitter** or a **reflector**. The former emits light energy into the environment, while the latter reflects the light energy of emitters and other reflectors.

The traditional method of computing radiosity has been to calculate all of the interactions between all of the patches. This method involves two steps that take into account a **form factor**, which is determined by the geometry of the surfaces in the environment. The calculation of the scene's geometry includes the distance of each patch from every other, the orientation of the surfaces in space, and whether there are objects blocking the transfer of energy from one part of the environment to another. The first step calculates the interactions of light energy between all of the patches, and determines the percentage of influence each patch has on the others. This step provides the form factor, which remains constant unless some object in the scene is physically moved. For instance, if the lights in a room are dimmed, the percentage of influence each surface has on every other remains the same as long as the geometry does not change. The second step calculates the colors of the surfaces in the environment that result from the light interactions calculated in the first step.

A technique known as **shooting** (named because it is used to *shoot* light energy from the patches) can be used to improve the efficiency of radiosity calculations. Although in a real lighting environment every surface has some effect on every other surface, the effects of some surfaces on others are minimal. The shooting technique ignores the influence of many of the patches on other patches for which the effects would not be obvious to the eye. Additionally, shooting combines the calculation of geometry and lighting, which would otherwise require separate calculations. Shooting is typically done in a step-wise fashion, computing the effects of the most significant energy contributors, followed by the next most significant, and so on. For instance, the first shoot might calculate the immediate effects of light emitters, and the second the effects of the walls closest to the light, and so on. Whereas the traditional method calculates the effects of every energy contributor, regardless of the amount of effect it has on other patches, shooting is complete after several calculations, having achieved a final effect that is close to the optimal one.

Unlike ray tracing, radiosity is **view-independent**: the location of the viewer's eye point is not a consideration in the algorithm. This means that once the lighting effects in the environment are calculated, they will remain the same, regardless of the location of the viewer's eye point. Thus, the calculation of the light in the environment can occur in advance, and the eye point can move around the scene in real time.

Radiosity is common in applications such as architectural computer-aided design that seek to simulate the diffuse lighting of building interiors. Because radiosity is view-independent, the architect can design true-to-life renderings of every room in an entire building, have the computer system calculate the lighting, and then let the client "walk through" each room by watching the computer screen.

Radiosity and ray tracing can be combined to produce both specular and diffuse results in the same environment. For instance, a room with diffuse lighting may nevertheless have a highly reflective floor that will produce specular highlights to some degree, even in diffuse lighting. Some applications use radiosity techniques for the non-reflective surfaces, and ray tracing for the reflective surfaces for ultimately realistic results.

Texture Algorithms

Surface textures can be applied to a solid model—via a **texture mapping** algorithm—to simulate real-world textures, such as wood grain, tile patterns, and stone. Applying surface textures with texture mapping is conceptually similar to adhering wall paper to a wall surface: we can select a 2-D texture, size it to the three-dimensional surface, and map it to the object, either by superimposing it or wrapping it around the 3-D surface. This makes it possible to cover a large area efficiently with a uniform pattern and avoids considerable computational overhead. Note that this 2-D technique is not entirely accurate for three-dimensional objects. For instance, an object cut from materials such as wood or marble should show an internal grain or texture. New work in texture volumes is addressing this issue.

One such method of creating 3-D textures is called **texture definition**. We are just beginning to see realistic results from algorithms that attempt to create fuzzy textures such as fur and wool. Dr. James T. Kajiya and Timothy L. Kay of the California Institute of Technology developed a method that defines a surface to be textured in a grid and uses each square as the basis for a texture element they called a **texel** (reminiscent of pixel).

The lighting algorithm used is similar to the Phong algorithm, except that it simulates lighting around thin strands in the textured surface, producing hair-like or fur-like results. Techniques such as this one, which is based on both volume-rendering and ray-tracing technologies, will make it possible in the future to dramatically improve the realistic quality in scenes that illustrate people, animals, and other complex textured surfaces.

Particle Systems

Particle systems, an advanced algorithm for treatment of non-polygonal surfaces, provides a method of describing surfaces and textures as amorphous as smoke and fire for dynamic, moving pictures. This algorithm deals with collections of tiny particles. More than 100,000 particles may be used, each with its own dynamic properties that can be manipulated to achieve the desired effect. These properties include position, speed, and direction of movement, size, shape, color, transparency, and duration of life.

As many of these properties can be manipulated as the application developer chooses, although it is most efficient, computationally, to keep several properties constant (such as size and shape) and to change those that are most important in a realistic, animated rendering. Because it would not be feasible to control the position of each particle in a complex scene, particle system algorithms typically cause many of the transformations (movement) of the particles, as well as other miscellaneous effects, such as their distribution, to occur randomly.

The controlled factors depend upon the substance the program seeks to simulate. For instance, the lifetime of smoke particles would be much shorter than the lifetime of fog particles. To compute the appearance of the scene, the program uses ray-tracing technology to determine what the eye sees on the screen at each pixel, in each frame.

Virtual Reality

Virtual reality technology seeks to eliminate the disparity between the inherent limitation of viewing an image on a monitor and actually experiencing it. The graphics monitor is able to display only a portion of the area that could potentially be viewed by the user. Regardless of how realistic the graphical environment might be, or how interactive, it resides on a monitor in front of the viewer, and the viewer is largely removed from the graphical experience. Figure 6-5 illustrates a person's field of view, and positioned within that field of view is the approximate viewing space provided by the computer display.

Figure 6-5   The field of view of human eyes, and the field of view of the average workstation display.

Imagine being surrounded by a rich, simulated environment in which you are able to guide your own course and your own activities, just as you do in real life. Virtual reality technology provides the user with such an environment, including a realistic field of view and the capability to move in all directions and to progress through the environment at will. It achieves this aim by attaching parts of the computer to the user: the user puts on a set of body gear containing electronic sensors and a graphical display that enable the user to fully experience a graphically-defined environment.

Many vendors are currently researching and creating their own versions of virtual world electronics. In a representative system, the user dons a special "data glove" and head gear with goggles that provide communications with the graphics system. The goggles provide the user with stereo views of the virtual world. Sensors in the helmet and data glove provide information to the system about the user's location and movements. As the user moves within the environment, transformations occur to update the user's view.

Virtual reality is still a very young technology. However, potential virtual reality applications for the future include both the practical and the fantastic. Some of the proposed applications include:

- An aid to the handicapped, enabling users to experience what they otherwise could not experience, due to physical limitations.

- A visualization tool for practicing difficult disciplines, such as tap dancing and martial arts.

- A simulation environment for places that are inaccessible to humans because they are too remote, too hot or cold, too dangerous, or too small. For example, a surgeon could use a micro-surgery application to make decisions based on a simulated walkthrough of the patient's body or could even perform the surgery in the simulated environment.

It has been conjectured that we will one day have the freedom to create our own personal realities with this technology. Your simulated environment might be a tennis match with your favorite tennis pro, an African safari, or a walk on the moon.

Conclusion

This chapter introduced the lighting model and its uses in several lighting methods that range in sophistication, as well as several advanced techniques for creating complex and realistic computer-generated environments. As computer graphics matures, new algorithms and techniques continue to be developed, so that even textures as defiant of geometry as hair and fur are now being simulated in computer graphics.

Thus far, the topic of transformations—or changes to pictures and scenes—has been discussed intermittently. Chapter 7 discusses the process of performing transformations in more detail, and introduces the viewing pipeline, the collection of events that occur as a picture is created, modified, and displayed on the graphics monitor.

An Introduction to Computer Graphics Concepts

Modifying and Viewing Pictures

This chapter discusses methods of transforming objects in size and in space, and introduces the **viewing pipeline**—the set of procedures involved in producing and displaying pictures on the graphics system. Topics include:

- Moving and modifying objects

- Moving the eye point

- Viewing in 2-D

- Viewing in 3-D

Moving and Modifying Objects

In Chapter 4, the "The Eye Point in 3-D Space" introduced the concept of the synthetic camera, which enables the application to draw objects in one position, and the eye point to move around them. This is one method of creating the appearance of movement in a graphical scene. The objects themselves can also be moved to new positions and angles, and many applications require movements and changes to the orientation of objects on a regular basis. The most realistic effects can be obtained by combining both movement of the camera (eye point) and object movement, as this essentially simulates real life.

Note that because the viewer remains stationery in front of the computer screen, it is not always detectable as to which is moving—the object or the camera. For instance, if there is only one object, such as a carousel, appearing to rotate in space before the viewer, and there is no other point of reference, it might not be clear whether the object was rotating, or the camera was traveling around it. However, if there was a background to the scene, such as a fence and a tree, these would remain in the same location if only the carousel moved, but would change orientations if the eye point moved. Also, if the scene employs direct light sources, points of light on the objects in the scene will appear to move across the objects if the objects are moving, but if only the eye point moves, the points of light will remain with the same objects.

Operations that move or re-orient objects are called **transformations**. These operations **translate** or change the locations of objects, **scale** them up or down in size, and **rotate** them to new orientations in space—operations that have very high computational requirements.

To move, rotate, or scale an object, the user makes a request of the application. The application interacts with the hardware to make these changes using a transformation algorithm that modifies the coordinates of the object through multiplication or addition, depending upon the transformation type. Transformation algorithms use **transformation matrices** that condense the mathematics of the operation into a compact form, enabling the application to make the changes to object coordinates efficiently. The hardware computes the change in the object using the matrix for that transformation and the new values indicated by the user's input.

The mathematics of modifying objects are transparent to the user, who makes requests for transformations through the application interface. To resize an object, for instance, the user might be able to manipulate slider bars in the application window that increase or decrease the size of an object. If the graphics system includes a dial box, the user typically can move, rotate, or scale an image by turning one of the dials (or "knobs"). The application can implement a different use for various dials so that each dial performs one of the basic transformations.

Translating

To translate an object means to move it to a new location on the screen. Also known as **panning**, translation creates an effect somewhat similar to the movement of a video camera across a scene. Computing a translation involves a matrix that represents the translation **offset**, which is the amount of space, at each vertex, that the object will be moved from its current location. The object is translated by that amount on each axis. For instance, if the user moves an object in 2-D, and the translation offset is 4, 2, each vertex coordinate in the object will be translated by 4 units to the right and 2 units up. Figure 7-1 illustrates a 2-D square translated by 4, 2.

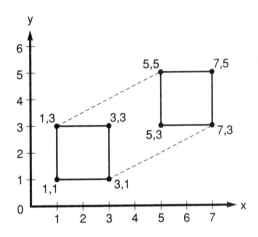

Figure 7-1   A translation in 2-D by an offset of 4, 2.

In 3-D, the concept is similar, except that there must be an offset for the coordinate in z as well. Figure 7-2 illustrates an object in 3-D translated by an offset of 2, 3, 4. This means that each of the object's coordinate points is moved to the right by two coordinates on the x-axis, up by three coordinates on the y-axis, and farther from the viewer by three coordinates on the z-axis.

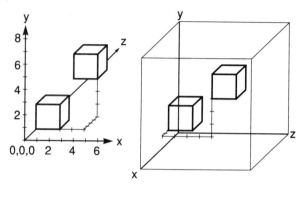

Cube vertices		
Front face	Before	After
	x,y,z	x,y,z
	1,1,0	3,4,4
	3,1,0	5,4,4
	3,3,0	5,6,4
	1,3,0	3,6,4
Back face	1,1,2	3,4,6
	3,1,2	5,4,6
	3,3,2	5,6,6
	1,3,2	3,6,6

Figure 7-2   A cube before and after translation with an offset of 2, 3, 4. Two views illustrate the same translation.

In this figure, two views are shown: a frontal view and a side view. The frontal view illustrates three-dimensional space as illustrated in most graphics texts. The side view here provides a second perspective to illustrate that the z-axis is perpendicular to the plane created by x and y, and to clarify the translation in the z-dimension. (One could think of the eye point shifting from the first view shown to the second view.) The table lists the coordinates of the cube's vertices before and after translation.

Scaling

Scaling produces an effect that is similar to the zooming of a camera lens—increasing or decreasing the size of objects—and for this reason, scaling is sometimes called **zooming**. Scaling an object to a new size involves a multiplication matrix that represents the scaling factor by which an object will be increased or decreased. This factor is multiplied by the coordinates of each vertex in the object. If the proportions are to remain the same, the scale factor must be the same for x and y (2-D), or for x, y, and z (3-D) and for each vertex coordinate. A number less than 1 decreases the scale, while a number greater than 1 increases the scale. Figure 7-3 illustrates an object in 2-D and an object in 3-D, each scaled by a factor of 3.

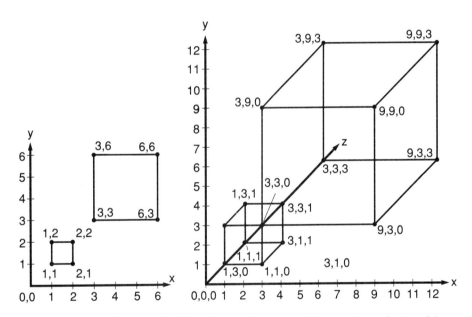

Figure 7-3   A 2-D object and a 3-D object, each increased in scale by a factor of 3.

Note that scaling also translates an object to a new location, because the object is not centered at (0, 0). Most applications will compensate by defining some other "origin" for the object about which the object is scaled.

Rotating

Rotations are handled very differently in 2-D and 3-D. A rotation in 2-D might be conceptualized better as a *pivot* than as a *rotation*, because 2-D rotations occur around a single point on the flat x, y-plane. Figure 7-4 illustrates this with an analogy to the hands of a clock face. The hands (the 2-D objects) can be rotated clockwise or counter-clockwise about a point. In this case, the point of rotation is the origin of x and y.

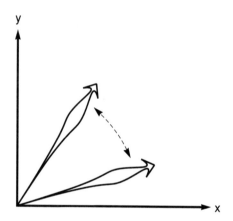

Figure 7-4   A rotation in 2-D.

In three dimensions, rotations occur not around a single point, but around a specified axis. Figure 7-5 illustrates a cylinder rotating on each of the three axes. For 3-D rotations, the application passes user input to the hardware, which uses a rotation matrix to compute the angle of rotation about a point or axis.

An Introduction to Computer Graphics Concepts

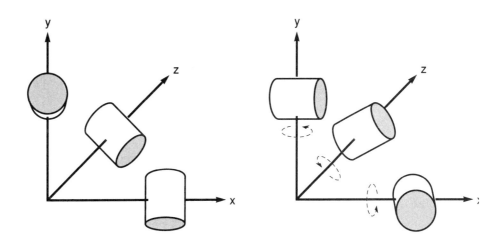

Figure 7-5   3-D rotations of a cylinder on the x, y, and z axes.

Viewing in 2-D

When objects are drawn, modified, and displayed, a series of events takes place that transforms the picture data "behind the scenes," so that changes occur quickly and unnoticeably. These events are called the **viewing pipeline**. The various stages in the viewing pipeline involve separate coordinate systems for the user, the software, and the hardware. When an object or scene is to be displayed, the separate coordinate systems are mapped to one another. This process defines the orientation of the object or objects in space, and, if the synthetic camera is employed, the position of the eye point as well. The calculations required by the steps in the viewing pipeline are intensive, particularly if the eye point or the positions of the objects in the scene change continuously.

The remainder of this chapter is devoted to a discussion of the major steps in the viewing pipeline. It first covers the viewing pipeline for 2-D graphics and then for 3-D.

Model Coordinates

In the graphics system, communications must occur between the user, the graphics library, and the graphics hardware. Part of the job of the graphics software is to provide the user with a logical workplace, and to translate user input into data that can be displayed in pixels on the hardware. It would be awkward for the graphics user to describe an object in pixel units. Not only are they non-intuitive units of measurement for any imaginable application, but they also vary in shape and dimension from one hardware device to another. If applications described objects directly in pixels, they would not work consistently on dissimilar hardware devices. For these reasons, the **model coordinate** system and the **world coordinate** system have been devised for the user.

Model coordinates form a coordinate system that is applicable to a single graphical object. For instance, if the object is a model of a toy, it might be logical to use a model coordinate system defined by inches or centimeters. Each object in a scene is defined by its own model coordinate system, which means that each object potentially has a unique measurement system. Figure 7-6 illustrates two portions of an object that were created in separate model coordinate systems. Ultimately, these separate parts must be combined into one coordinate system, in like units of measurement.

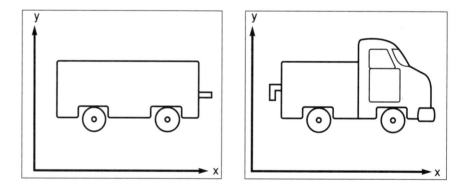

Figure 7-6   Two parts of a toy truck in separate model coordinate systems.

World Coordinates

The world coordinate system, or **world space**, is the space where the separate model coordinate systems for a picture are combined into one. All objects in a scene are defined in model coordinates, and they are mapped to world space and placed in relationship to one another. The measurement system in world space depends upon the particular application. For instance, the toy truck model might best be described in inches.

An Introduction to Computer Graphics Concepts

Some portion of the world space data are placed in a **window**. This is not a window in the window system, but rather a region that defines the area of interest within the world coordinate system. In Figure 7-7, the separate model coordinates for the truck are mapped into a window in world coordinates.

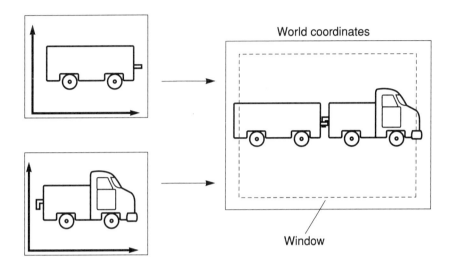

Figure 7-7   Model coordinates for the toy truck mapped to world coordinates.

Clipping

Mapping the picture to the world coordinate window determines what portion of the picture will be displayed. Anything that falls outside of the world space window must be discarded via a **clipping** algorithm. Clipping relieves the graphics library of the work of drawing primitives that fall outside the window boundaries and removes any distracting parts of the scene to help the viewer focus attention on the intended portion.

Clipping is a time-consuming process for the graphics system, because it requires a series of tests. The tests determine whether each primitive is entirely within the window (no clipping required), partially within the window (primitives are clipped and the visible portion displayed), or entirely outside the window (external primitives are discarded). The clipping test algorithms must be efficient because there may be thousands of primitives to be considered for possible clipping in a single drawing, and if the object or the eyepoint is moving, clipping is an on-going process. Two common clipping functions (described above) require fewer calculations and are aptly named: when primitives are entirely outside the window, the process is called **trivial reject**; when they are entirely within the window, it is called **trivial accept**.

Device Coordinates

The coordinate system that underlies the raster graphics display, defining the raster grid, is a two-dimensional space described by x and y axes. Its measurement system describes the parameters of the device's display surface in pixels. These coordinates are called **device coordinates**, or **device space** because they are specific to the particular graphics display device.

Normalized Device Coordinates

Device coordinates and world coordinates are interfaced by another coordinate system belonging to the graphics library called **normalized device coordinates (NDCs)**. The normalized device coordinates provide a device-independent coordinate system (with values between 0 and 1), and transforming these to device space is a matter of multiplying the values by the resolution of the display device. The world coordinates are mapped into the NDC space, which defines the **viewport**: a portion of the display surface selected as the viewing area. Figure 7-8 illustrates the toy truck clipped to the world coordinate window and then mapped to the viewport window in NDC space.

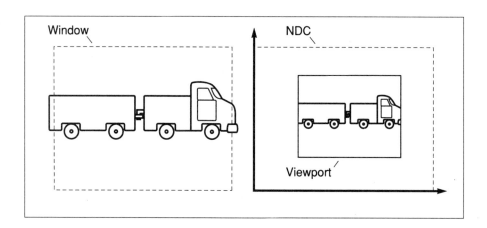

Figure 7-8 Mapping a window onto a viewport.

After the world coordinate window is mapped to the NDC viewport, the NDC space is mapped to the pixels in device space. Several viewports on the viewing surface can be designated for separate views of the same object. Figure 7-9 illustrates the toy truck in three viewports.

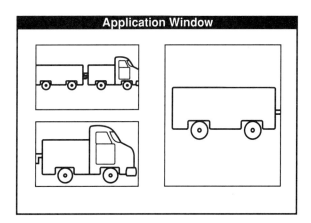

Figure 7-9   The toy truck in three separate viewports.

For review, the entire 2-D viewing pipeline is as follows: first the image is created in model coordinates. Next, the application maps the model space to a window in world space. The window is then mapped to a viewport in normalized device coordinates. The viewport is mapped to the device space and to the actual display device. Finally, the pixels for the picture are determined, a color is written to these pixels, and they are illuminated on the display device.

Viewing in 3-D

The viewing pipeline is essentially the same in three dimensions as two. However, because of the complexity involved in portraying three dimensional images on a two-dimensional surface, two steps must be added to the viewing pipeline for 3-D: one in the clipping phase and one at the time of display.

Clipping in 3-D

The 3-D image must be clipped in height and width, just like a 2-D image, but it must be clipped in the depth dimension as well. Clipping in the depth dimension of the 3-D view volume is called **z-clipping**, because the algorithms are concerned with the space along the z-axis. A **clipping plane** is used to define the limits of the available image area. The library must assess which parts of the objects pass partially or fully through the clipping planes and then clip these areas from the view volume before drawing. Figure 7-10 illustrates a cylinder in 3-D space. The front and back clipping planes indicate the limits of the display area.

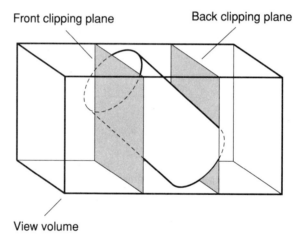

Figure 7-10 An image in the view volume, limited by front and back clipping planes.

Projection

For 3-D coordinates to be mapped to the 2-D coordinates of the display surface, the three-dimensional image must be **projected** onto a two-dimensional view plane. Projections reduce the dimensions of the image for display on the 2-D computer screen, much like a picture from a camera produces a 2-D image of a 3-D scene. This can be conceptualized with rays, called **projectors**, that emanate, point by point, from the 3-D image to the 2-D surface.

Projections can be performed in parallel or in perspective. Figure 7-11 illustrates a 3-D image being projected to the 2-D viewing surface with **parallel projection**, whereby the projectors are parallel to the z-axis, and with **perspective projection**, whereby the projectors meet at a vanishing point.

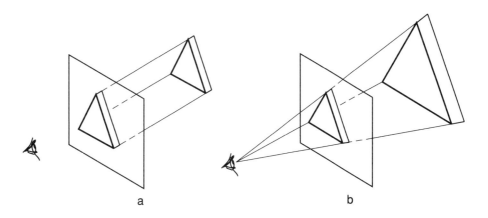

Figure 7-11 Parallel projection (a) and perspective projection (b).

Depth clipping is especially important with perspective projection. Recall that there is no limit to the conceptual dimensions of the view volume. The graphics library cannot truly draw objects all the way to infinity: at some point the scale is so small that when the image is translated into device space, the library cannot draw more than a clump of points and lines that result in a spot on the screen. Limiting the depth of space available for drawing relieves the library from attempting to draw objects that are too distant, in world space, to be discernible to the eye. Moreover, it prevents the hardware from making unnecessary calculations.

After clipping and projection from 3-D to the 2-D view plane, the picture is mapped to the viewport and then to the pixels in screen space.

The whole 3-D pipeline now occurs as follows: the objects are defined in model space, and the scene is composed by mapping those objects to 3-D world coordinates; the scene is clipped against the view volume for height, width, and depth; it is projected from 3-D to a 2-D view plane; the image is then mapped to the viewport in normalized device coordinates and then into the system's physical device coordinates.

Conclusion

This chapter discussed picture transformations and introduced the separate coordinate systems for the user, the graphics software, and the graphics display hardware. The coordination of all of these events occurs in the graphics library and application database, which are discussed in detail in Chapter 8.

Graphics Libraries

This chapter discusses the graphics library, and introduces several industry standard libraries in common use. Topics include:

- Picture updates and the graphics library
- Display list libraries
- Immediate mode libraries
- Industry standard libraries

Picture Updates and the Graphics Library

Picture transformations require updates to the data describing the picture. The picture data must remain intact, somewhere in the system, until updates occur, the data are revised, and the new picture is drawn. Although picture data are always stored by the application database, some graphics libraries also store copies of the data for intermediate updates.

Graphics libraries that store a copy of the picture data are called **display list** graphics libraries. Because they store, or "retain," a copy of the data, they are sometimes called **retained mode** libraries. Graphics libraries that do not store their own data are called **immediate mode** libraries.

Figure 8-1 illustrates the relationship of the application and the display data for both display list and immediate mode.

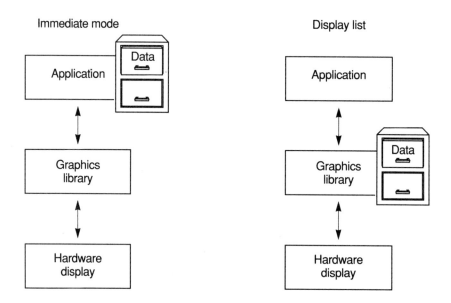

Figure 8-1   Immediate mode and display list handling of graphical data.

The "display list" is the display data for the picture, such as the edge list for a wireframe model or the face list for the surface model, as well as any attributes (picture characteristics) that describe the color and other qualities of the picture. The display list is essentially a subset of all of the data in the application database, restricted to the data required for drawing the picture.

Application developers typically use display list libraries when it is cumbersome for the application to interact with the application database each time the user makes a change to the picture data. To operate more efficiently, the application extracts the graphical data from its database and puts it into the library's display list.

An immediate mode library, by contrast, is driven directly from the display data in the application database. Application developers generally use immediate mode libraries when it is less efficient to extract the picture data for intermediate handling than to make changes directly to the database. This is particularly true when the changes to picture data are so extensive that the data are almost completely different from one frame to the next. In this case, the application database must be updated constantly, and it does not serve to keep a copy of the picture data in a display list.

An Introduction to Computer Graphics Concepts

Each method has its advantages, and some graphics libraries have both display list and immediate mode capabilities, enabling the application developer to choose the mode that is appropriate for the application. For instance, an application such as a mechanical design and analysis program that requires regular, expedient changes to the same picture data might be best designed with display list capabilities. However, in many animation applications, scenes are pre-generated and then displayed rapidly without modification. In this case, the immediate mode design might be more appropriate.

Hierarchical Display Lists

In a display list library, picture data are organized into either a **hierarchical** or **linear** display list. In a hierarchical display list, the elements of the picture can be **nested**, and nested elements can inherit attributes and position from the elements above them in the hierarchy. The two methods are designed for different types of accessibility. These methods are analogous to two different designs for filing cabinets. The hierarchical display list is analogous to a filing cabinet in which major categories contain subcategories, which contain additional subcategories. Figure 8-2 illustrates a hierarchical filing system for food categories.

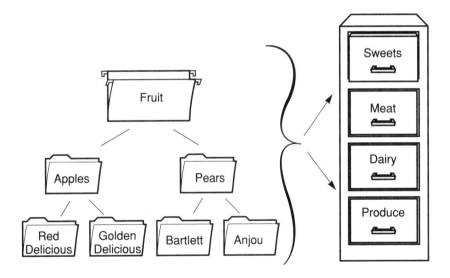

Figure 8-2   Filing cabinet in the hierarchical display list style.

In this system, a large folder contains the category of "Fruit." Within that large folder, additional folders contain smaller folders titled "Apples," "Pears," and so on, each of which contain separate documents describing their varieties. If we move the Fruit folder from a cabinet drawer titled "Sweets" to a cabinet drawer titled "Produce," every folder and document within the Fruit folder moves with it.

The display list hierarchy, sometimes called a tree, provides a method of logically grouping picture elements. Picture components directly above others in a tree are called **parent structures**, and the grouped elements branching from them are called **child structures**. **Ancestors** are all the structures between a child structure and the initial structure (including the initial structure) at the top of the hierarchy. In Figure 8-2, "Apples" is a child of Fruit, and the parent of "Red Delicious" and "Golden Delicious." Apples, Red Delicious, and Golden Delicious are all **descendants** of Fruit, as are the Pears.

Hierarchical structures can inherit attributes and transformations from their parent structures, which can simplify the task of manipulating cohesively grouped portions of objects.

Figure 8-3 illustrates a robotic arm designed with a hierarchical display list application. Movement of some portion of the object, such as the hand, depends on and reflects the movement of other parts of the object, such as the wrist, forearm, upper arm, and body.

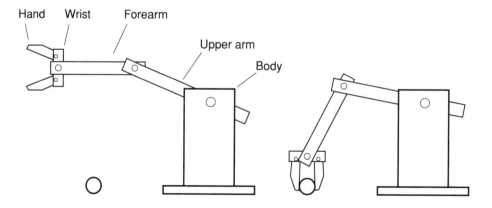

Figure 8-3   Movement of a robotic arm.

An Introduction to Computer Graphics Concepts

Linear Display Lists

In linear (or "flat") display lists, picture components are unrelated. A flat display list is analogous to a filing cabinet that has no major categories or subcategories. Every document in the cabinet might simply be filed alphabetically. The user of this file system has accessibility to each component in the system, without affecting the other components. For instance, moving or removing the file on anjou pears is a simple task that has no affect on any other document. Figure 8-4 illustrates a filing cabinet that is analogous to a linear display list.

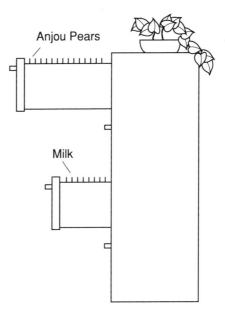

Figure 8-4 Filing cabinet in the flat display list style.

Benefits of Display List Graphics

In a display list system, the graphical data have been gleaned from all of the data in the application database and stored in the display list for fast access. Thus, display list graphics is especially useful for applications that require frequent modifications to small portions of a large database.

Viewing an object from multiple angles is especially easy in applications that use a display list-based library. For each view, the application simply requests a new "camera angle" from the graphics library. The application does not need to reproduce all the graphical objects in the new view, because they are already in the graphics library's display list.

Display list elements can also be edited, enabling users to modify pictures interactively.

Limitations of Display List Graphics

With display lists, much of the control of the graphical data is given to the graphics library rather than to the application developer. In hierarchical display lists, for instance, while the hierarchy makes the display list data manageable, it reduces the developer's flexibility for manipulating small portions of pictures without affecting other aspects of the picture.

Another drawback to display lists is that updates to the local storage must be synchronized with the application database; thus updates to data must occur in two places rather than one, which requires more computer memory.

Benefits of Immediate Mode Graphics

Some graphics users may already have a well-established graphics storage method associated with the application database. In this case, an immediate mode graphics library will preserve the user's investment in the existing graphics setup, and will enhance the system in use. Immediate mode gives the application programmer the freedom to design the structure of the graphical data.

Many applications do not benefit from display list graphics. For instance, some applications require the display of large amounts of data that are already stored, such as data that have been captured by satellite or that were digitized from a photograph. These applications are better suited to immediate mode.

Finally, because the graphical data are not duplicated in a local display list, storage requirements and database update problems are minimized.

Limitations of Immediate Mode Graphics

One drawback to immediate mode is the database traversal necessary to reconstruct the picture. If any damage to the picture occurs, caused by the overlaying of another window or an error message, the application must restore the picture by accessing the data from the application database. In the application database, the graphical data are generally interspersed with other data. Depending upon the amount of data stored in the database, in addition to the data that specifically describe a picture, accessing the picture data can be time consuming.

Library Standards

The graphics industry has standardized several graphics libraries that are used by graphics programmers industry wide. Two standards organizations that review and approve proposals for standards from the electronics industry and a variety of other industries are the American National Standards Institute (ANSI) and the International Standards Organization (ISO). The standardization of tools or interfaces such as graphics libraries enables many developers to build products based on a standard API (application programmer's interface), available on the majority of platforms from different vendors. Additionally, the developer is able to work at a higher level, to use the tools offered by the high-level programming interface, rather than writing very low-level code. This enables developers to work more efficiently and provides them with an open environment in which they can develop various products using one consistent and familiar library.

Standard graphics libraries are **vendor independent**: they are not exclusively designed to run on a graphics system of a particular make but can be used on many different system types. Typically, the hardware vendor develops an implementation of the standard that is optimized for that company's hardware.

For examples of immediate mode and display list libraries, this section introduces two library standards. **GKS**, the Graphical Kernel System, can operate as a flat display list system, or it can operate in immediate mode. **PHIGS**, the Programmer's Hierarchical Interactive Graphics System, is designed to be a hierarchical display list system.

The GKS Graphics Library

GKS, the Graphical Kernel System, is a sophisticated graphics library used for 2-D graphics applications. The flat display list feature of GKS groups related primitives and picture attributes into **segments** that can be scaled, rotated, and translated. These segments can be combined, in a linear fashion, to form whole objects, and can be copied into other segments that are being created, thus reducing calculation time. The segments cannot be nested in a hierarchical manner, however, which means that they are independent of one another and do not inherit attributes or movement from other segments. Thus, when the application requests a translation of an object from one part of the screen to another, each segment must be translated individually to its new location.

There are a number of operations, in addition to the transformations listed above, that can be performed on GKS segments, providing the user with special control during application run time. **Control visibility** is an operation that makes segments visible or invisible. **Control priority** establishes segment priority with respect to other segments. This affects the order in which segments are drawn when a picture is created. **Control detectability** determines whether or not a segment can be selected by a device such as the mouse (and its pointer). **Delete segment** removes segments in all associated graphical windows. **Highlight segment** distinguishes segments in some way, making certain segments more visible in the application.

Segments in the GKS display list cannot be edited. For instance, if one of the polygons in a segment composed of two polygons is to be changed, the data in the entire segment must be regenerated: the new polygons must be defined in a new segment and posted to the display list, and the old segment deleted from the display list.

GKS can also operate in immediate mode in which case no segments are created or displayed. Although the application developer has control over the design and manipulation of the graphical data, the application handles all updates through the application database. GKS can operate in both immediate mode and display list simultaneously. For instance, the application might define a background image, such as a map, in a display list, and an image such as a small plane flying over the map, in immediate mode. This makes it possible to update the map image efficiently (for instance, if the user wants to pan across the map to track the flight path of the plane) by modifying the existing display list, and to regenerate the image of the plane in its travels via immediate mode.

The PHIGS Graphics Library

PHIGS is a sophisticated graphics library for 2-D and 3-D graphics applications that provides numerous services to the application developer including input handling and data archiving. However, for the purpose of this book we will limit the discussion to its graphics output capabilities.

PHIGS organizes its display list data in hierarchical structures that comprise the primitives and attributes describing a picture. These structures can be grouped to reflect their position in the hierarchy and can be shared among separate structures, reducing the amount of data to be stored. Once a structure is defined, it can be treated as a single unit and can be **referenced** for repeat occurrences in other parts of the hierarchy. A bike wheel consisting of a hub, spokes, and rim, for instance, can be designed as a structure and then referenced for the drawing of the second wheel. The reference does not contain the actual graphical data, but points back to the structure that defined it. This technique eliminates redundancy, and reduces the storage requirements of the picture.

PHIGS structures are stored in a database called the **central structure store** (CSS). The CSS contains the structures that comprise primitives, attributes, and references to their substructures. The hierarchical grouping in the CSS of primitives and structures enables PHIGS applications to create dynamic movement as transformations are inherited by the substructures invoked by their ancestors.

PHIGS is designed for use in applications requiring smooth animation, such as simulation programs, molecular modeling and many mechanical computer-aided design (MCAD) applications. PHIGS structures can be modified and edited interactively, and transformations and updates can be performed in the PHIGS library's display list containing only the information required to display the picture data. This means that updates are handled efficiently by the application, and changes to the application database can be deferred until time allows.

PHIGS PLUS

PHIGS PLUS, an extension to PHIGS, is a proposed standard currently in review by the ISO and ANSI standards organizations at the time of this writing. The *PLUS* in PHIGS PLUS is said to be an acronym for the multi-lingual phrase *Plus Lumière Und Surfaces*.

PHIGS PLUS augments the output primitives in the existing PHIGS standard by introducing a corresponding set of extended primitives with additional information and attributes. These extensions support lighting, shading, and depth-cueing. Additionally, PHIGS PLUS adds a new set of sophisticated output primitives, including triangle strips, quadrilateral mesh, Non-Uniform B-spline Curves, and Non-Uniform B-spline Surfaces.

X and PEX

PEX is an acronym for **PHIGS Extension to X**. We have discussed window systems in a general way, but we have not yet discussed the X Window System or the X Library. This section introduces the X Window System and then provides an overview of the enhancements provided by the PEX protocol.

The X Window System

The X Window System was developed by Project Athena at the Massachusetts Institute of Technology, and has since become a de facto standard through its wide adoption in the computer industry. This distributed window system is designed to work efficiently across a local area network via a communication **protocol**.

The X Consortium was later formed to make the X Window System available to the entire computer industry and to encourage further development and enhancement by others in related fields. The X Library (commonly called **Xlib**), is a system programmer's interface to the X protocol. Xlib prepares information **packets** that are essential to the communication between the host computer and the application, relieving the application and the system programmer of this burden.

The **X11** protocol—the current version of the X Window System—essentially defines how window applications communicate with the local display system, providing implementors with a consistent, yet policy-free foundation for development of window system tools and applications on heterogeneous (dissimilar) workstations.

The Xlib packets are groups of specific pieces of information required between the application and the display systems. The packets provide the communications that make it possible for a local display-equipped system to present windows and two-dimensional graphics from software running on multiple, distributed application hosts.

The PEX Extension

PEX, the PHIGS Extension to X, is a direct enhancement to the X11 protocol to support the 3-D graphics standard. The development of the PEX protocol extension and the subsequent effort to implement a widely available version of the PEX extension-handling server and PHIGS/PHIGS PLUS library was sponsored by the X Consortium at MIT. It was implemented by a group at Sun Microsystems, Inc. and is sponsored under the direction of the X Consortium by its following members: Data General Corp., Digital Equipment Corp., Evans and Sutherland, Fujitsu Limited, Hewlett-Packard Company, International Business Machines, Network Computing Devices, Open Software Foundation, Solbourne Computer Inc., Sony Corp., SpectraGraphics, Stardent Computer Inc., Sun Microsystems Inc., Tektronix Inc., and Unicad Inc.

PEX enables the distribution of advanced graphics applications to occur across the network, through PEX protocol support of PHIGS and PHIGS PLUS. The PEX protocol supports interactive 2-D and 3-D drawing capabilities, as well as hidden line and hidden surface removal methods, advanced curve and surface primitives, and lighting and shading. Additionally, PEX enables applications to take advantage of graphics accelerator hardware on the display server system. Figure 8-5 illustrates the relationship of the window system to PHIGS.

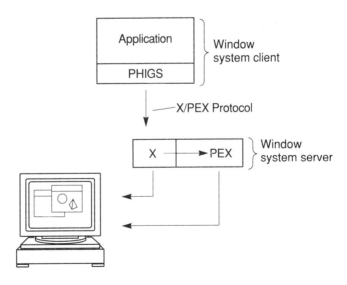

Figure 8-5 The PEX protocol model

PEX enhances both PHIGS and X, by enabling X to support native 3-D graphics capabilities, while increasing the portability and accessibility of applications developed with PHIGS and PHIGS PLUS. Currently proposed as an industry standard, PEX will potentially minimize some of the software development, maintenance, and documentation burdens for application developers and users of X window systems.

Conclusion

This chapter introduced four methods of handling graphical data in the graphics library and application database: editable hierarchical display lists, editable linear display lists, non-editable linear display lists, and non-editable immediate mode. Additionally, the chapter introduced several industry standard graphics libraries that enable developers to write applications in familiar environments across separate vendor platforms.

We have developed a large working vocabulary of terms for the components, techniques, and concepts employed in creating pictures with computers. Computer graphics is a part of a larger set of technologies related to electronic image generation, processing, and management. Chapter 9 introduces the world of imaging technologies, of which computer graphics is a part. It also discusses several advanced techniques in computer graphics and other imaging environments.

An Introduction to Computer Graphics Concepts

Image Processing and Visualization

This chapter introduces special topics in imaging technologies that complement computer graphics and use related techniques. Topics include:

- Image processing
- Image reconstruction
- Scientific visualization
- Volume rendering

Imaging

Imaging is a broad category encompassing a variety of computer science technologies, including computer graphics, designed to generate or process images. Imaging also includes fields such as **image reconstruction**, a technology used primarily in medical imaging, that enables users to produce viewable images from sources such as X-rays; **scientific visualization**, a technology that seeks to expedite the process of analyzing scientific data through graphical representation; and **volume rendering**, a method of creating solid volumes from data such as medical image reconstructions.

Image-Processing Technology

For many applications graphics and image processing are companion technologies, and it is important to know what distinguishes them and how each is used. One of the foremost distinctions between imaging and computer graphics, is that while "graphics" generally refers to computer-generated images, "image processing" refers to pictures that have been captured from external sources, either as digital data or as hard-copy images that must be converted to digital data for computer display. Examples of some of these sources are photographs, space probe photography, **remote sensing** data (satellite and aerial images), computerized axial tomography (CAT-scan), magnetic resonance imaging (MRI), and ultrasound.

Image processing involves techniques that modify visual data. The goal is typically to enhance or clarify images that can otherwise present extremely abstract visual information and to use the results to promote further analysis. For example, one might want to take data describing the planet Saturn, digitize it into data that can be displayed with a graphics CRT, and enhance the planet's rings. This can be accomplished with specialized software that provides tools for detecting edges, highlighting certain aspects of the image, filtering out "noise" such as non-image-related color streaks, and so on.

Like computer-generated pictures, digitized images are displayed on raster graphics workstations, and they require hardware with multi-bit display memory. And, as in graphics, images are stored in the frame buffer, in bits corresponding to pixels that collectively represent the image on the raster display. However, the application database for image processing stores image information much differently. This is because the image data are collections of *values* rather than geometric data. Each bit/pixel relationship represents one of many values that, when combined, form the image on the screen. In graphics, pictures are created from data that describe the geometry of images. For example, a rectangle in a graphics picture is defined by its four vertices, and can be manipulated using this information alone. However, a similar rectangle in a digitized image is known to the system as a bunch of pixels, with binary color or gray-scale values; the system has no way of knowing that those pixels constitute a rectangle.

The volume of data describing scanned images tends to be much larger than data describing computer-generated pictures and can require as much as 8 megabytes of storage, or even more, for a single, medium-sized image. For this reason, and because the operations performed on digitized images tend to require a great amount of compute power, image-processing applications usually require acceleration for acceptable performance.

Image Sources and Applications

Any photograph can be digitized into binary data for display on a raster monitor and processed with image-processing equipment and software. Processed photographs are used in a variety of applications, such as advertising, mapmaking, and urban planning.

In the past, remote sensing equipment produced photographs, but increasingly this equipment produces digital data for direct raster representation, eliminating the step of digitizing. Applications for these images include the study of heat and radiation from the earth or ocean, the monitoring of changes in geographical areas such as volcanic and seismic regions, the study of the ozone layer, and military surveillance.

Applications in **earth resource management** (see "Earth Resource Management" in Chapter 10) use raster graphics systems, and often a combination of image-processing techniques and computer graphics techniques, to view and analyze data. As an example, an oceanography research group could analyze satellite images of an ocean region after processing the images for clarity and then develop computer-generated graphical models of the flow of ocean currents for further analysis of the same region.

In medical fields, X-rays are perhaps the most common medical imaging source. These are produced with electromagnetic radiation that is capable of penetrating tissue to obtain data from internal organs. Computed axial tomography, or CAT-scan technology, uses X-rays to produce data for reconstruction into 2-D cross-sectional slices. CAT-scan technology is concerned with the **density** of the tissue at each ray. These data are gathered, computed, and projected onto the detector device for reconstruction. Magnetic resonance imaging (MRI), a related technology, produces data by electronically sampling a tissue area that has been simultaneously charged with electromagnetic radiation and a magnetic field. This technology is used to detect abnormal cells in cross-sectional images of muscle, tissue, and bone.

CAT-scan and MRI data are reconstructed into two-dimensional pictures for analysis of patients' internal organs. Medical professionals can detect abnormalities before resorting to the more invasive measures of surgery, and they can plan surgical procedures more precisely.

Image Reconstruction

In medical imaging, image data are captured with one of the several methods and must be **reconstructed** into viewable images before image-processing techniques can be applied. An entire research and development technology exists around the reconstruction of images. Medical imaging is one of the primary uses of this technology, but the same techniques can also be used to create image data in other environments.

Image data are gathered by issuing radiation through an object and projecting the radiation rays onto a detection device. Each ray is a one-dimensional sample of an internal portion of the object. The collected projections form a two-dimensional pattern that can be reconstructed into a cross-sectional **slice**, which can then be viewed and analyzed. Figure 9-1 illustrates this process.

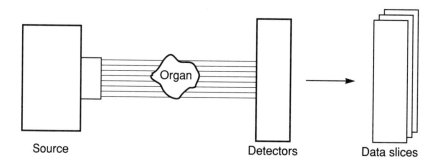

Figure 9-1 Rays projected through an organ to produce 2-D data for reconstruction.

Image-Processing Techniques

The goal of image processing is to improve, modify, or restore images so that they are more easily understood and analyzed. Two of the primary categories of image-processing techniques are **image restoration** and **image enhancement**. The method used depends upon the type of image data collected and the application's needs.

Image Restoration

Image restoration techniques repair damage or degradation in images and restore them to an approximation of the ideal appearance of the image. There are a number of ways for artifacts to be introduced into images. A degradation of some degree is inevitable as images are captured and transferred to printed or electronic media, because we are reducing the "resolution" of real life into two-dimensional space. Further degradations can occur if the camera is not properly focused, if the subject matter is a moving object, or if there is a high level of atmospheric activity that causes distortion as the image is captured. Images can also degrade as they are transferred from hard copy to electronic media.

One common image restoration technique is **filtering**, a method that smooths out unwanted features, such as cloudiness or **noise**—artifacts that distort the image. Figure 9-2 illustrates a digitized image before and after filtering. In the first image, the data were affected by electronic noise. An interference was introduced into the data as the image was digitized for computer display, and then propagated across the image, appearing as a series of stripes. The second image is the restored version, after filtering.

Figure 9-2   Photograph before and after filtering.

Image Enhancement

Image enhancement techniques process images in ways that do not necessarily reflect the original ideal of the image. The goal is usually to modify an image so that certain features are more prominent, rather than to return the image to a likeness of the ideal image. Some image enhancement techniques accentuate certain features and others enhance a particular aspect of an image through sharpening of contrasts, edges, or features, or modification of some features to obtain a new effect. As an example, in mapping applications a digitized photo might be processed to increase contrast or to apply **pseudo colors** to a grayscale image by assigning certain colors to specific types of terrain.

In medical imaging, image enhancement techniques are often used to improve the quality of the reconstructed image so that the physician can analyze vascular, muscular, or skeletal structure more easily, and can thus detect abnormalities.

Figure 9-3 is a split image that illustrates an original chest X-ray before and after image processing. The right half of the image shows the results of a detail enhancement technique, known as the **Wallis filter**.

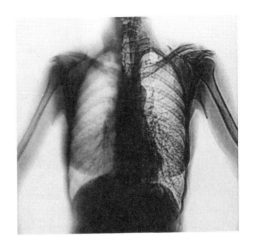

Figure 9-3   Chest X-ray before (left) and after (right) image enhancement.

Thresholding

Thresholding is one of several image enhancement techniques commonly used in the medical field. This technique is used to create greater contrasts in the image to eliminate features that are not critical to analysis. For instance, a particular thresholding algorithm might convert all pixels below a certain gray-scale value to black and those above the threshold to white, thus highlighting specific image features, such as blood vessels.

Figure 9-4 illustrates a heart that has been injected with iodine prior to the imaging process. The X-ray highlights several types of tissue in the heart.

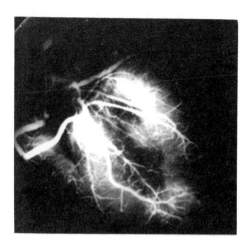

Figure 9-4   Heart X-ray before thresholding.

The analyst can perform several levels of thresholding to further increase contrast. For instance, an initial thresholding might enhance the blood vessels while reducing the prominence of other tissues in the organ, but may not reveal the location of a suspected abnormality. Thus, a second level of thresholding can be applied to bring out even stronger image contrasts. Figure 9-5 illustrates a first level and second level of thresholding. In the final image, a break in the image of the blood vessel on the far left may indicate a possible constriction.

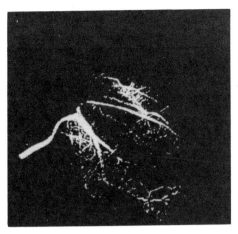

Figure 9-5   Heart X-ray after one level of thresholding, and after a second level of thresholding.

Image-Processing Hardware Requirements

Because imaging pictures are not predefined in terms of geometric primitives that can be manipulated in isolation, displaying and transforming the visual data makes greater demands on the processing hardware than does the manipulation of computer-generated data.   The data describing an image tend to be more complex and must be stored virtually pixel by pixel. All of these data must be managed when the image is displayed and manipulated. As a result, the capabilities of the processing hardware must be sophisticated and fast.

Typically, the computers used for this kind of data manipulation have been powerful "super computers" or workstations with special-purpose image-processing add-on boards, but this is changing. Industry trends are moving in the direction of high-quality, high-resolution, multi-processing workstations that have the power to handle great volumes of image data.

Scientific Visualization Technology

Scientific visualization is a diverse field that uses graphics and other imaging technologies in a variety of applications designed to aid scientists in analyzing complex data.

Scientists gather research data from many sources—from space exploration, lab experiments, electronic seismic equipment, soil and oceanic testing equipment, and so on. This abundance of data presents a formidable task to the scientist seeking to analyze and derive accurate conclusions and results. The methods for collecting the information usually generate great amounts of mathematical data that do not inherently present clear meaning.

As an example, one metropolitan city gathers samples of air quality in its urban area every ten minutes throughout the day, every day of the year. These samples are broken down by air temperature, carbon monoxide, and sulphur dioxide levels and are then accumulated as numerical data. With the use of visualization software tools, a user can construct a 2-D or 3-D graphical color model from the data and thus view the results of an entire year's data collection in one sitting. Obvious patterns emerge about the times of day and the times of the year that emissions are highest, enabling the user to form hypotheses about the effects of temperature and weather upon the gas accumulation levels.

Visualization efficiently communicates ideas and synthesizes the meaning of repeat patterns in numerical data, enabling the user to quickly eliminate from consideration all data of little or no importance and to concentrate on data that present concrete, meaningful information.

Simulation

Simulation is a method of scientific visualization used in testing and training environments. Motion dynamics in technical and scientific fields can provide simulated flight programs, animation of mechanical movements and fluid flows, and simulation of chemical reactions.

Fluid Flow Dynamics

Many design problems are difficult to solve without a physical model or prototype. Traditionally, some aspect of the machinery under consideration, if not the entire model (an automobile, an airplane, or a submarine, for instance), had to be built and tested. If the testing revealed problems, another iteration of model building and testing would occur, and so on, at great expense in time and money.

Computer simulation enables a design engineer to interactively select design options and examine the results. As an example, a fluid flow analyst might compose a mathematical 3-D computer model of an aircraft's engine and run it through a testing program that simulates the activity in the engine's combustion chamber. The analyst is able to view the process of gas combustion entering the turbine stage and the resulting heat variations. Temperatures must be high for combustion to be efficient, but not so high that they exceed allowable temperatures for the metal parts. The simulation enables the analyst to find the optimal design for efficient combustion at the optimal temperatures. Though a model of some type may still need to be built and tested, several iterations have been eliminated, and the product development has been reduced from many months to perhaps several days. This has important implications for cost, quality, time to market, and competitiveness. Figure 9-6 illustrates the process of developing solutions based on analysis of graphical representation of data.

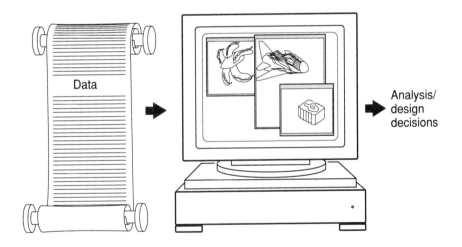

Figure 9-6   Simulation and analysis pipeline.

Volume Rendering

Volume rendering is a relatively new field that incorporates image processing and high-end 3-D graphics for visualization of **volumetric** data in scientific research environments. Volumetric data describe an object or space in three dimensions, but unlike the picture data described in the discussion of 3-D computer graphics, volumetric data do not originate from geometry. As with the 2-D image-processing applications discussed earlier in this chapter, volumetric data are typically digitized from external sources. To work with the data, we can display it on the raster monitor, determine the locations of specific objects or features on the bitmap, and then manipulate the data in groups of pixels.

Volume-rendering techniques enable scientists, engineers, and analysts to create 3-D solid volumes from a variety of data sources, including medical imaging sources, remote sensing equipment, and seismic data. Because the data from sources such as CAT-scans are inherently 2-D, volumetric data can be created by combining the two-dimensional image slices into three-dimensional volumes. Figure 9-7 illustrates a series of cross-sectional data slices that compose a 3-D volume.

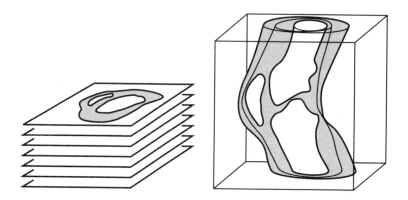

Figure 9-7   Data slices combined to create a 3-D volume.

Voxels

In volume rendering, a 3-D volume is computed as a structure composed of volume elements, or **voxels**. Voxels are analogous to pixels in that they are the smallest elements in a viewing coordinate system, except that voxels are three-dimensional, and they describe a solid 3-D viewing space, rather than a flat viewing surface. For display, the 3-D voxels that are visible to the eye point must be mapped to corresponding 2-D pixels, in a manner similar to the projection of 3-D graphical data to the 2-D viewing surface discussed in "Projection," in Chapter 7. Figure 9-8 illustrates occupied voxels in a volume.

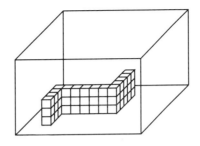

Figure 9-8   A voxel volume.

Surface Modeling

There are two methods of rendering volumes from volumetric data: **surface modeling** and **direct volumetric rendering**. The surface modeling method essentially reconstructs the surface of a 3-D volume from the 2-D sample data slices generated by a source such as MRI. With this method, surface modeling first employs an image-processing algorithm, called **edge detection**, to define the parameters of the structures in the image data. It then defines three-dimensional surfaces and contours based on the edges of various shapes. Next, these surfaces can be described in terms of geometric primitives, and the voxel faces can thus be treated with the familiar geometric surface-rendering algorithms developed in computer graphics.

Direct Volumetric Rendering

The direct volumetric method creates a *solid* 3-D volume, rather than a *surface* that defines a volume. The voxels in the volume are treated as occupied or unoccupied cells. Those that are part of the image data are occupied and are visible, and those that are not part of the image data remain unoccupied and are not shown.

With this method, it is possible to slice through the volume at any angle to expose its internal composition. This method is useful in analyzing the internal features of medical imaging volumes and geographic data volumes from seismic regions. Figure 9-9 illustrates a cube with an **oblique** (not perpendicular to the x, y, or z planes) cutting plane that has sliced into the volume. Ideally, the application program allows the user to cut away at any angle to expose the internal data.

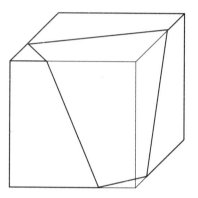

Figure 9-9   An oblique slice through a volume.

Scientific data are often conveyed in multi-dimensional formats. For instance, in addition to the x, y, and z dimensions, the user might want to illustrate data such as time, temperature, or pressure. Color Plate 9 illustrates a fluid flow model created with a data set that simulates seismic information and a volume-rendering software package. The volume itself is a three-dimensional model of a hot and a cold tectonic plate. A fourth dimension is depicted with the pseudo-colored layers that portray the turbulent temperature distribution between plates. To illustrate temperature distribution over time, the user could superimpose that data over the same model and thereby depict a fifth dimension.

Ray Casting

Ray casting, a technique used in direct volume-rendering methods, makes it possible to render multiple objects with color and transparency in a volume data set. With this algorithm, rays are cast through the volume—one ray for each pixel in the display surface—and the program collects information about the volume from along each of the rays. Figure 9-10 illustrates rays cast from the eye point through a volume.

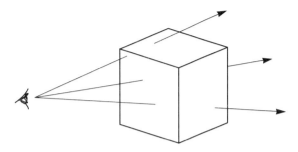

Figure 9-10 Ray casting through a volume.

The information gathered along the rays can be classified into specific substances appropriate to the particular volume, such as muscle and bone in a CAT-scan. The application user defines a range of values for each substance to be compared with the data gathered by the rays. As the rays gather data samples from the volume, the program determines the number of voxels each substance occupies as well as the visual quality of that substance. This information is sent to the shading model, which calculates the color of the screen pixel.

Conclusion

This chapter introduced several imaging environments that have developed separately from computer graphics, or, in the case of volume rendering, have developed directly out of advances in computer graphics. These technologies, combined with the computer graphics algorithms discussed throughout the book, provide a vast range of image creation and processing techniques and capabilities that answer the needs of many users.

So far, we have discussed graphics and imaging applications as particular graphical concepts pertain to them. Chapter 10 introduces a variety of application environments for computer graphics and other imaging technologies. Additionally, it discusses the software needs of each of the application areas.

Applications

This chapter discusses some of the many applications for computer graphics and computer imaging. Topics include these predominant application environments:

- Electronic publishing

- Electronic design automation

- Architecture, engineering, and construction

- Mechanical computer-aided design

- Graphics and animation

- Geographical information systems

- Earth resources

- Medical imaging

- Chemical engineering

Application Environments

With sophisticated graphics libraries and interactive graphics, image processing, and visualization tools, graphics system users are solving a vast range of design, engineering, and scientific analysis problems. This chapter presents an overview of the most prevalent application environments, their software needs, and some of their success stories. Chapter 11 discusses the application requirements from a hardware perspective.

Electronic Publishing

Electronic publishing applications are used across a wide spectrum of industries, including marketing firms, newspaper and magazine publishers, and the high-tech aerospace, automotive, telecommunications, and manufacturing industries.

In the past, company brochures and ad layouts had to be created by hand or handled by specialized design firms, but with the advent of on-line desktop publishing systems, many industries have begun to produce their publications in-house. Electronic publishing software enables users to prepare "camera-ready" copy for periodicals, advertisements, brochures, newsletters, presentations, and sales charts.

Most electronic publishing applications require text and 2-D graphics. Software packages that provide these features range in complexity from fairly basic word processing packages with a user interface for producing text and simple drawings, to highly sophisticated packages with a variety of fonts, drawing capabilities, and layout tools for fast page makeup.

Desktop publishing not only expedites the process of producing camera-ready materials for publication, but it can reduce publishing budgets as well. One magazine publishing company purchased a composition package for generation and layout of text and graphics, and a database for storage. The staff produces, edits, and finalizes copy layouts on the computer. They are then able to print the copy, overlay halftones, and send them to a printing service. The company saves nearly $10,000 annually in editing costs by producing and altering text and graphics on-line.

An example illustration from an electronic publishing application is shown in Color Plate 10.

Electronic Computer-Aided Design (ECAD)

The electronics industry uses computer graphics systems and software extensively. Engineers in the aerospace, automotive, instrumentation, telecommunications, and semiconductor environments use electronic computer-aided design (ECAD) and electronic design automation (EDA) software in the design of computer chips and printed circuit boards.

The EDA and ECAD environments rely almost exclusively on two-dimensional primitives, such as 2-D vectors, 2-D polygons, and text. In the most basic applications, these primitives are used in designing essential schematic drawings, but the software needs of users in this industry extend to the highly complex. In the higher level applications, 2-D primitives are used in designing simulation models that require sophisticated graphics libraries and large databases for storage and retrieval.

An ECAD system can increase the productivity of circuit board designers, providing efficient software tools such as an overlay process by which many layers of the various materials are placed in their prospective locations, one by one. The result is a simulation model that can be tested for viability before the design is actually implemented.

Common EDA applications include the design of printed circuit boards, layout of integrated circuit chips, analysis and testing of designs, and simulation of electrical circuits and power flows.

An example illustration from an electronic design application is shown in Color Plate 11.

Architecture, Engineering, and Construction (AEC)

The AEC industry is one of the fields most actively converting to graphics systems and software for its design solutions. The spectrum of applications in this field includes the design of interiors, commercial structures and landscapes, power plants, and telecommunications networks. Most notably, AEC applications encompass civil engineering projects, such as highways, railways, bridges, airport runways, and dams.

AEC applications require sophisticated graphics libraries and large database storage to produce drawings for its diverse customer base. Architects and engineers in this field typically use computer-aided design (CAD) software packages. The specially designed software aids the designer with many tasks, from the layout of a structure's foundation to the design of its wiring systems and the analysis of stress forces on the structure.

Many AEC applications use 2-D primitives exclusively, including 2-D lines and polygons for blueprints, and text for specifications. These elements enable the architect or civil engineer in traditional design environments to produce the familiar two-dimensional layouts.

Now, with the increasing availability of low-cost graphics systems and software, this field is moving rapidly in the direction of producing three-dimensional likenesses of proposed structures. This strategy has several benefits. It enables the designer to analyze the structure for potential problems, such as awkward placement of pipes, and to increase drawing accuracy. Additionally, it enables clients virtually to "visit" the complete structure before it is built. The 3-D viewing transformation capabilities of the graphics system provide the client with views of the structure's interior and exterior from many angles.

In design workgroups (client/server environments), networked CAD systems offer special advantages. Software stored on a main database can provide many components of the design process (design elements, clip art, and so on). Members of the workgroup contributing to the same design can check that design file out of the database, complete their portion of the work, and check it back in. And, if bookkeeping software is part of the database management system, each member of the workgroup can access inventory and billing information.

In architectural design, where a client usually awards a contract to the lowest bidder or to the firm that can promise the quickest turn-around time, competition is intense. With the use of high-performance workstations and a sophisticated CAD package, one firm was able to promise a one-year turn-around time for the design and reconstruction of a 20-building complex that had been destroyed by fire. The company, which had recently upgraded from personal computer systems, found that they were able to produce drawings two to three times faster, and were thus able to complete the project in only 10 months.

An example illustration from an AEC application is shown in Color Plate 12.

Mechanical CAD (MCAD)

In mechanical engineering environments, it is becoming increasingly common for computer graphics systems and mechanical computer-aided design software to replace traditional methods of producing mechanical parts, tools, vehicle components, and complex machinery.

Mechanical CAD application software simplifies the mechanical design process, enabling the designer to build new products efficiently from established models by specifying the new dimensions. Editing existing drawings is also more efficient with on-line, interactive design modification tools, and fast storage and retrieval mechanisms.

MCAD applications tend to be highly sophisticated, both in 2-D and in 3-D. Some graphics systems offer specific 2-D and 3-D hardware support for MCAD applications. In low cost systems, where 2-D and 3-D hardware support is not available, the MCAD application handles all graphics operations in software. Thus, the user sees the same picture on different platforms, and the performance scales with the cost.

Three-dimensional wireframes provide a way of viewing parts and structures from all sides swiftly and interactively. For more realistic, "final product" representations, designs can be rendered further with solid-colored surfaces, company emblems, and other features. Rendering techniques that are especially important in 3-D MCAD applications include hidden surface removal algorithms, lighting, and reflective surface-modeling methods.

Mechanical designers are finding that MCAD solutions and electronic networking decrease their time to market and improve communications with their manufacturing colleagues. One automotive design firm in Massachusetts has reduced both design time and costs by 25 percent. Additionally, electronic links to the manufacturer in Tokyo enable designers and engineers to share design plans and communicate changes quickly.

An example illustration from a mechanical computer-aided design application is shown in Color Plate 13.

Graphics and Animation

Graphics and animation applications serve many industries, including such fields as video technology, commercial and non-commercial art and advertising, cartooning, and scientific simulation.

As with all of the application environments discussed so far, the sophistication of graphics and animation applications ranges from the simple to the highly complex. Animation applications, for instance, include simple two-dimensional cell-type animations for Saturday morning cartoons, the fast-moving 3-D "flying logos" used for advertising news and sports programs, and sophisticated flight simulation programs for pilot training.

These applications are handled very differently from one another. With the cell animations, the animation sequence typically is performed by creating each frame of the animation sequence in advance, and then rapidly drawing each one on the computer screen. By contrast, flight simulation models, which are the most computationally intensive of the animation applications, operate interactively. None of the movements are precomputed. Instead, the program must simulate altitude gains and drops and craft movement in any direction or angle, show the terrain below as seen by the pilot at all times, and indicate the entrance of other aircraft into the plane's airspace—all interactively, and upon demand by the application.

Cartoon and the flight simulation applications use 2-D and 3-D solid-filled polygons almost exclusively. The flying logos used on network television are typically a mix of both wireframes and solid polygons. Applications that we might not think of as "animations"—for example, simulations of physical phenomena such as fluid flows and power flows—also use both wireframes and solid polygon representations. When simulation speed is critical but solids are not required for realism, wireframes can be used for the fastest transformations; solid polygons can be used when solid flows are critical to accurate analysis. Similarly, graphics users in design environments often benefit from the initial use of wireframes, which can be created, drawn, and transformed much more quickly than solid surfaces. It is common for design application users to create wireframes for this reason, and then convert them to solid surfaces for the final effect.

An example illustration from a graphics application is shown in Color Plate 14.

Geographic Information Systems (GIS)

Geographic Information Systems are database systems that combine census data, demographic information, and information related to geographic locations to create information tools for mapping and data analysis applications. Applications in GIS range from methods of determining the best location for emergency services in a particular community to studying the likelihood of finding ancient ruins among a sampling of geographical locations.

These applications primarily use libraries of 2-D output primitives for creating maps and other graphical analysis tools, but like the AEC and MCAD environments, 3-D applications are becoming increasingly common. The GIS community can benefit greatly from graphical tools such as 3-D contour maps and representation of multi-dimensional data sets, which can describe

An Introduction to Computer Graphics Concepts

geographical environments in three dimensions and classify the data in the environment—such as forestation or population density—with another dimension.

Some GIS applications simplify traditional methods of obtaining demographically related marketing data. Historically, demographics on the typical profile of a product user, in a particular locale, have been organized in lists of numbers and had to be painstakingly analyzed. GIS applications can now make use of accessible and intuitive graphical methods of viewing and analyzing such data.

GIS applications are also used for cultural research. With a database of information about a geographical area in Utah, the U.S. Geological Survey was able to target locations most likely to be the sites of historic native American villages. The agency compiled existing knowledge about several villages and noted the common characteristics. These villages had commonalities such as a particular elevation and a view of the surrounding terrain, a particular distance from a water source, a soil type, and the availability of a source of pine nuts from a specific pine species. Additional sites were tested for the presence of these characteristics with a mapping program, and the maps were overlaid on the graphics workstation. The project was extremely successful: of the locations pinpointed as probable historic sites, 85 percent were found to have supported native American populations.

An example illustration from a GIS application is shown in Color Plate 15.

Earth Resource Management

Study of natural resources and interpretation of geologic and seismic data are some of the most common earth resource management applications. As with GIS applications, mapping data, combined with information databases, provide users with a meaningful method of exploring and analyzing large amounts of data. Earth resource management differs from GIS in that the data used are exclusively scientific as opposed to census and demographic data. Additionally, earth resource applications are moving rapidly into the use of both 3-D data and the volumetric rendering of solids.

Common applications in earth resources are productivity modeling for oil wells, coal and gas exploration, terrain modeling, and seismic testing. Many such applications require both image-processing and graphics systems. For instance, with both graphics and image processing capabilities, the scientist can take data from various sources, such as computer-generated models and digitized satellite photographs, display them on a graphics workstation, process and analyze both data sets, and compare the results.

Earth resource management applications are becoming increasingly common in environmental studies. Several research groups use modeling systems to test the likelihood of global warming as a result of various influences. First, they gather recorded satellite data from around the world that describe ocean temperatures and atmospheric circulation. Using these data, they create models to represent atmospheric conditions, oceanic conditions, and land conditions, such as snow and soil. The models are structured on a grid and display information relating to latitude, longitude, and altitude. At the grid intersections, real-world data are applied, indicating such variables as wind, weather, and solar radiation. These models can then be run through a simulation to test the result of increased levels of carbon dioxide and other influences.

An example illustration from an earth resource application is shown in Color Plate 16.

Medical Imaging

Medical imaging is one of the oldest imaging technologies and one that has sparked great interest in the rapid development of special techniques for visualizing complex scientific data. Imaging capabilities in this field, traditionally confined to flat, 2-D formats, are now taking advantage of some of the advancements in other imaging areas, such as computer graphics. Many medical imaging applications still rely solely on image-processing techniques for data enhancement and analysis. Increasingly, however, as medical professionals seek improved visualization capabilities, the medical field is turning to special volumetric graphics capabilities for producing and transforming complex solid volumes.

Software requirements in medical imaging include image-processing packages, high-end 3-D graphics tools, and volume-rendering capabilities for creating and transforming volumes from 2-D data slices. Rendering requirements in volume-rendering applications include sophisticated three-dimensional solid surfaces, 3-D solid volumes, and transparencies.

In radiology, medical professionals are finding that 3-D rendering aids analysis and treatment planning. Although the 3-D volumes provide the same information as the 2-D images, the radiologist may find it much simpler to

An Introduction to Computer Graphics Concepts

communicate the diagnosis and the location of the problem to the surgeon. The 3-D representation can be rotated in any direction to new views. A tumor located at the base of the skull, for instance, might be more easily analyzed from a profile view of the skull than from a frontal view. The user can rotate the volume rendering of the skull to view the area of interest and can then zoom in on specific areas for closer examination.

The radiologist can also use computer graphics to model a radiation beam, and can superimpose the model of the beam over the volume model to plan where the radiation beam should go and what intensity it should be.

One medical center plans to treat cancer with proton beam accelerators that use radiation to destroy a tumor without harming surrounding tissue. A computed tomography scan provides 70 gray-scale images of the malignant area. The analyst processes the samples to assign colors to various components, to produce a composite image, and to plan treatment based on a simulation. The graphics workstation not only provides the display surface and simulation power, it delivers the proton beam as well. The doctor uses the mouse to position the angle of the beam and then applies the appropriate dosage based on the simulation and treatment planning.

An example illustration from a medical imaging application is shown in Color Plate 17.

Chemical Engineering

Chemists seeking to analyze the reactions of molecules to various chemicals are able to model these reactions with high-quality graphics software and sophisticated multi-processing hardware. Animation techniques enable the chemist to simulate vibrating bonds and to employ color changes in the molecular model to simulate chemical reactions. Because of the immense data files that are typical in this field and the transformation requirements of the animations, molecular modeling is at the highest end of the graphics scale; it requires more sophisticated software and faster hardware than any applications discussed so far.

Typical applications in this area include crystallography (a science dealing with crystallization and the forms and structure of crystals, typically used in pharmaceutical research), genetic and protein engineering, molecular modeling, and drug design.

One chemical laboratory is seeking to identify and quantify proteins that seem to play a role in killing brain cells during a stroke. When strokes occur, protein patterns change. The chemist separates the proteins by charge and molecular weight, deposits them on a gel, and then digitizes an image from the gel onto the workstation. The chemist then makes a comparison of treated and untreated gels, enters the data into a database, and analyzes the results. The analysis may someday help determine the precursors to strokes and possibly aid in their prevention.

An example illustration from a chemical engineering application is shown in Color Plate 18.

Conclusion

This chapter discussed several application environments and their software needs. Many of these applications require special hardware support to run efficiently. It can be difficult to wade through the jargon associated with computer graphics performance and acceleration. Chapter 11 discusses the hardware needs for the application areas described in this chapter, introduces the concept of the benchmark, and discusses methods of accurately judging graphics performance.

Performance Metrics

This chapter discusses the importance of accurate performance metrics, and introduces the concept of the standardized benchmark. Topics include:

- Graphics acceleration
- An application scale
- Price/performance trade-offs
- Judging Performance
- Benchmark Standards

Graphics Acceleration

We have discussed acceleration of computer graphics images to some degree throughout this book. Graphics accelerators off-load many of the graphics operations from the otherwise overburdened central processing unit (CPU). As the sophistication of graphics, image processing, and visualization applications increases, so does the need for sophisticated accelerator hardware.

Anyone in search of a graphics system can easily become overwhelmed by the options for graphics system acceleration, and especially by the figures that graphics hardware vendors use to characterize the performance of their systems. This chapter seeks to provide insight into some of the issues governing graphics system performance. Additionally, we will discuss performance numbers, how they are derived, and more importantly, how the potential buyer can judge the validity of performance data.

The Application Scale

Chapter 10 discussed a wide range of application environments, each with varying software and hardware needs. It is important for the application to be able to rely on hardware support that is commensurate with its demands. Applications such as charts and graphs for business graphics produce 2-D graphical output that requires high-quality software but does not need dedicated graphics hardware processing support. By contrast, a scientist analyzing data in a volumetric display program needs extremely high-level hardware processing power in addition to excellent visualization software.

Application hardware requirements can be divided into several categories, based on the types of primitives that they typically use. Figures 11-1 and 11-2 compare the software and hardware needs of the range of applications discussed in Chapter 10. Figure 11-1 illustrates the range of graphics software categories and their importance to each application environment, and Figure 11-2 illustrates the hardware acceleration required to support them.

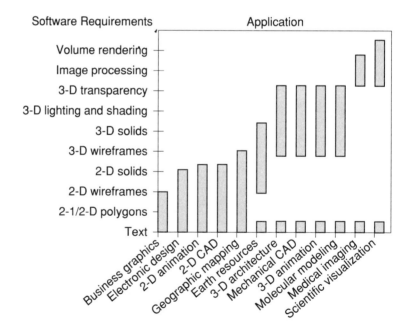

Figure 11-1 Application software requirements.

An Introduction to Computer Graphics Concepts

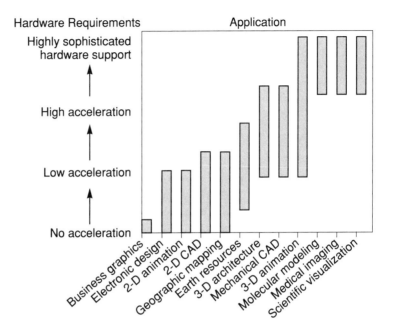

Figure 11-2 Application hardware requirements.

Price/Performance Trade-Offs

User productivity is directly related to the efficiency of the graphics system, and, as we have discussed, it is important to think about the application requirements at the time the system is purchased. Because computer images are generated and processed using data that describe shapes and colors in numerical values, sophisticated graphics and imaging applications require graphics hardware that can process numbers at high speed. By the same token, applications that do not need to render solid three-dimensional data sets or do fast transformations of complex pictures do not necessarily need sophisticated high-performance hardware. And, because of the costs involved in accelerating graphics, it is important to gauge the application's needs carefully. At any level of graphics sophistication, we want the best performance for the price.

The lowest cost solution is for all graphics operations to occur in software, using the main CPU of the system. This requires no specialized hardware for acceleration. Although this is completely appropriate for business graphics and many desktop publishing applications, the MCAD designer would find this method painfully slow.

For most of the applications listed in Figure 11-1, some amount of hardware acceleration is important for adequate performance. The increase in performance that graphics accelerators provide varies according to the amount of processing they are designed to perform. Simple accelerators speed up the drawing of 2-D lines and polygons. More complex accelerators increase the performance of higher level geometric tasks, such as the display of 3-D vectors and polygons, the lighting and shading of objects, and the display of higher resolution pictures. The increase in the amount of specialized graphics hardware, and hence performance, has a direct effect on the price of the graphics system.

Questions to ask in analyzing the application needs:

- Does the application require drawing speed, visual realism, or both?

- What rendering features are important?
  - 2-D polygons (wireframes/solid surfaces)
  - 3-D polygons (wireframes/solid surfaces)
  - Lighting/shading
  - Solid volumes

- What are the application's frame buffer requirements?
  - 8-bit indexed color?
  - 24-bit true color?
  - Z-buffering?
  - Double-buffering?

Questions to ask when considering the purchase of graphics hardware:

- Is graphics acceleration a part of the complete workstation configuration, or must that be purchased separately? (What is the cost differential if both options exist?)

- What level of graphics sophistication does the accelerator support?

An Introduction to Computer Graphics Concepts

- Will upgrades be available as technology advances?

- Do the applications for which the system is being purchased run on this particular hardware?

In addition to selecting the right performance for the application's needs, it is important to balance the capabilities of the CPU and the accelerator. If one of the components is slower or cannot handle the amount of data being generated, that component will become a bottleneck and slow down the whole system.

It is important to ensure that the application's most important operations are handled by hardware, and if possible, by a dedicated accelerator. In carefully analyzing the application's requirements and purchasing hardware acceleration for operations that are most important to the success of your work, you will gain the best price/performance ratio for your needs.

Judging Performance

Judging the performance of a graphics system and pairing appropriate performance to application needs involves understanding performance metrics. Graphics system performance is difficult to measure, and at this time no single method has been accepted industry wide. Currently, workstation vendors are creating their own programs for measuring graphics system performance and reporting numbers based on individualized metrics.

Benchmark figures, which are an attempt by graphics hardware vendors to qualify system performance, are the results of various performance measurement tests. The following sections discuss how benchmarks are derived, how they can be compared, some of the problems posed by the various measurement systems, and how the graphics industry is moving to solve those problems.

Benchmarks

Graphics system performance can be measured in a number of ways. Unfortunately, benchmark figures typically reflect the speed of low-level operations, such as the number of vectors or polygons the system can draw per second, or the number of raster operations the system can perform per second. Vendors typically publish *maximum* benchmark results over all the possible combinations of variables. These numbers may or may not be good predictors of performance for other combinations of attributes. For instance, a machine that performs well for one-pixel-wide vectors may not be the fastest for drawing 10-pixel-wide lines. Thus, these figures tend to ignore many other variables that affect graphics system performance as well as the spectrum of primitive and attribute types that a given application might require. This section addresses each of these issues in turn.

Measurement Variables

Many factors come into play as the application draws pictures on the computer screen. The viewing pipeline that transforms the picture from raw data into device coordinates for screen display varies among graphics libraries: some pipelines are much more complex than others. For instance, a graphics library (PHIGS, for example) which supports sophisticated features such as transformations, lighting, shading, and depth cueing, has a more complex viewing pipeline than one such as GKS, which generally supports flat-shaded, two-dimensional polygons. Each of the characteristics in the viewing pipeline is important to the overall performance of the application. However, because there are so many variables to negotiate, and because they differ among graphics libraries, it is difficult to achieve standard measurement across all potential graphics platforms.

Just as important as the viewing pipeline is the type of primitive the system is measuring. In a performance measurement of vectors, examples of variables that should be taken into consideration are the vector length, width, style, and orientation. For instance, it is important to note if the vectors measured are two-dimensional and align with the x and y axes, or if they are vectors of random orientation in three-dimensional space. While the two-dimensional vector-drawing capabilities are of use to specific applications, such as circuit board design, the three-dimensional vector-drawing figures are critical to applications such as mechanical computer-aided design in which complex 3-D drawings are the norm. Similarly, wireframes are generally much less taxing on the compute hardware than shaded polygons, and the performance numbers yielded by testing the drawing of one type of polygon are not valuable data for all applications. Thus, the conditions under which performance is tested greatly affect the benchmark results.

An Introduction to Computer Graphics Concepts

Benchmark Standards

The computer graphics industry is moving to establish standards for producing benchmark numbers. This strategy will provide more reliable and consistent performance data industry wide. Several standards committees are working on establishing a set of standards that will be applicable across the spectrum of application needs. These committees are composed of representative individuals from most of the major graphics workstation vendors in the industry as well as the two major graphics organizations: the Association for Computing Machinery Special Interest Group on Computer Graphics (ACM/SIGGRAPH) and the National Computer Graphics Association (NCGA).

TIGPE

TIGPE, the Technical Interest Group for Performance Evaluation, a non-profit group sponsored by ACM/SIGGRAPH, began the initial work of defining the problems associated with measuring performance across applications and data types. The TIGPE group defined four levels of graphics system performance:

1. The Primitive Level Benchmark, consisting of the low-level benchmark figures, such as vectors per second and polygons per second.

2. The Picture Level Benchmark, measuring frames per second, or the length of time it takes to draw a picture on the screen.

3. The System Level Benchmark, measuring interactive manipulation of objects on the screen, including rendering performance, as well as the effect of interactions between the system and the user via input devices such as the mouse and dial boxes.

4. The Applications Benchmark, consisting of the numbers generated by running specific user applications.

GPC

GPC, the Graphics Performance Characterization committee, a non-profit group sponsored by NCGA, endorsed the four benchmark levels developed by the TIGPE group and gathered funds to further develop the Picture Level Benchmark (PLB) as an industry standard.

The PLB is intended to provide a consistent method of measuring graphics performance. This method, which correlates to level two of the TIGPE requirements defined above, takes into account the important notion that graphics system performance is not reliably measured in a static environment. Real performance criteria, in environments where object movement is a part of the application, must consider animation for realistic performance measurements.

The PLB is a program designed to measure the actions that the user's actual application requires. The program runs on specific vendor hardware, which means that the potential purchaser is able to run specific applications on the hardware of vendors that participate in the benchmark standardization effort. The user provides the vendor with the picture data to be tested, and specifies the types of transformations required. To provide data that the vendor can use, the purchaser must first convert the application to a standard format, called the Benchmark Interchange Format.

Benchmark Interchange Format

The Benchmark Interchange Format (BIF) is a standardized file structure for specifying the geometry of a particular data set from a particular application as well as the user interactions to be performed. This standard enables the same data set to run on dissimilar vendor systems and promotes testing efficiency. The data need only be converted to this format once for testing on all vendor platforms.

Benchmark Timing Methodology

The Benchmark Timing Methodology (BTM) provides a method of measuring how long it takes to run the purchaser's BIF program and ensures that the viewing pipelines of dissimilar graphics libraries are measured in a consistent manner. The BTM provides the conditions and parameters necessary to determine the length of time it takes to run the requested benchmark.

Benchmark Report Format

The Benchmark Report Format (BRF) provides a standardized format for reporting benchmark results. This format provides the purchaser with a consistent data-tracking system for comparing hardware platforms. Because no two vendors' hardware platforms are alike, some may offer certain features that others do not. The BRF is a printout that informs the purchaser of the criterion used in the benchmark so that if a feature such as Z-buffering was not allowable, the user can take that fact into account in comparing hardware.

It is clear from this discussion that no single number—such as vectors per second—can adequately portray system performance. As performance measurement standards become the new way of doing business, the workstation vendor and the purchaser will be able to develop a cooperative arrangement to accurately qualify system performance, and to determine the best price/performance package for the user's needs.

Conclusion

This chapter discussed the graphics acceleration needs of a range of applications, and introduced benchmarks and the need for benchmark standards. Because the standards have not yet been fully adopted in industry, it is important to keep in mind that any non-standard approach to producing benchmark figures is subjective and potentially misleading.

For additional reading material on the growing field of computer graphics, please see the Bibliography, which lists a wealth of excellent texts on the subject.

Glossary

In this glossary, terms that are used in the text of definitions are *italicized* if they are defined separately under their own names.

absolute coordinates

A location relative to a coordinate system's *origin*. In *Cartesian coordinates* a two-dimensional point is known by its distance from the origin along the x and y axes, and a three-dimensional point is known by its distance from the origin along the x, y, and z axes.

accelerator

See *graphics accelerator.*

addressable point

The smallest coordinate point on the raster screen that can be addressed. Usually refers to a *pixel*, which can be individually addressed and illuminated by the display processing hardware. Raster displays were once named "all points addressable."

AEC

See *architecture, engineering, and construction.*

algorithm

A sequence of steps designed to solve a problem or execute a process such as drawing a curve from a set of control points.

aliasing

The jagged *artifact* in a line or in the silhouette of a curve that results from drawing on a raster grid. Aliasing occurs in all graphical images drawn on raster displays, but is especially noticeable in low-*resolution* monitors. The *sampling* frequency is a major factor in aliasing. See also *antialiasing* and *jaggies*.

ambient light

Non-directional illumination or surrounding light.

American National Standards Institute (ANSI)

An organization that reviews and approves product standards in the United States. In the electronics industry, their work enables designers and manufacturers to create and support products that are compatible with other hardware *platforms* in the industry. Examples are *PHIGS* and *GKS*. See also *International Standards Organization*.

animation

Simulation of motion through rapidly changing images.

ANSI

See *American National Standards Institute*.

antialiasing

An algorithm designed to reduce the stair-stepping *artifacts* (sometimes called *jaggies*) that result from drawing graphic primitives on a *raster* grid. The solution usually relies on the *multi-bit raster*'s ability to display a number of *pixel* intensities. If the intensities of neighboring pixels lie between the background and line intensities, the line becomes slightly blurred, and the jagged appearance is thereby diffused.

API

See *application programmer's interface*.

application

A software program specially designed for particular user needs or the specific use of a software program. Graphics applications are usually designed to enable the user to manipulate data or images, or to create images from data or from a library of shapes.

application developer

The person who creates an application for a particular user need.

application programmer's interface (API)
> The interface to a library of language-specific subroutines (called a *graphics library*) that implement higher level graphics functions. See also *binding*.

architecture, engineering, and construction (AEC)
> A computer graphics market requiring specialized applications that facilitate efficient planning, design, drafting, and analysis.

area sampling
> The determination of a pixel's color and intensity based upon the color and intensity of the pixels surrounding it.

artifact
> A visible error or oddity in a displayed image. *Aliasing*, for instance, is an artifact resulting from producing images on a *raster* grid.

ASCII
> (Pronounced *as-kee*.) American Standard Code for Information Interchange. The standard binary encoding of alphabetical characters, numbers, and other keyboard symbols.

attribute
> The property of an *output primitive* that determines characteristics such as color, line type, and line width.

back face culling
> Omitting the drawing of one or more backfacing polygons (which cannot be seen by the viewer), thus increasing drawing speed.

backfacing polygon
> A polygon with a *normal vector* that is pointed away from the viewer. Often the backfacing polygon is *occluded*, or hidden from view by opaque polygons that are closer to the viewer. If the surface is closed, the backfacing polygon can be omitted to save computational overhead, since the object will appear the same with or without it.

Bezier curve
> A curve created from endpoints and two or more control points that serve as positions for the shape of the curve. Often used in *MCAD* applications. Originated by P. Bezier around 1962 for use in car body design in France.

Bezier patch

A portion of a 3-D surface generated using the *Bezier curve* algorithm. Two 2-D Bezier curves are drawn through selected *control points,* and the 3-D curve is *interpolated* between them.

bilinear patch

A 2-D surface *patch* that can be warped into a 3-D surface. Some set of points in 2-D space forms the parameters of the patch, and these points are connected by straight lines. The patch shape is warped to the surface, but the lines themselves do not warp, and remain linear.

binding

Language-dependent code that allows a software library to be called from that computer language.

bit

Short for "binary digit." Indicates the smallest unit of information that is stored in a digital memory. Binary digits indicate two possible values: on and off. A single bit is represented in memory as 0 (off) and 1 (on).

bit block transfer

See *bit blt.*

bit blt

(Pronounced *bit blit.*) Short for "bit block transfer." A raster operation (*raster op*) that moves a block of bits representing some portion of an image or scene from one location in the *frame buffer* to another.

bitmap

The array of values in the frame buffer for a given picture, particularly in the case of monochrome (single-bit) displays. The term *pixmap* is often used for the array of pixel values in the raster in more complex gray scale or color monitors, which have more than one bit for each pixel in the raster display.

bit plane

The hypothetical two-dimensional plane containing a *bit* in memory for each *pixel* on the *raster*. For any raster image, there is at least one bit plane in *frame buffer* memory; each bit plane has a one-to-one correspondence of bits to pixels. There are additional bit planes for some raster systems. For instance, a 24-bit system has 24 bit planes. (The storage structure which represents the bit plane in memory is an array)

bounding box

A rectangular box aligned with the axes drawn around the smallest area that entirely contains a particular polygon or object. Often used in fill algorithms in which tests are made to find out which *pixels* are inside and which are outside a polygon. Also called an *extent*.

B-spline curve

A curve defined by a series of *control points*. The control points define a series of continuous *Bezier curves*.

byte

A grouping of adjacent binary digits (*bits*) operated on by the computer as a unit. The most common size *byte* contains 8 binary digits.

CAD

See *computer-aided design*.

Cartesian coordinates

A system named for French mathematician Rene Decartes. Cartesian coordinates form a coordinate system by which points, lines, and other *primitives* can be located. In 2-D, the coordinate system forms a single flat plane (the *x, y-plane*) upon which flat objects can be oriented in relationship to two axes (x and y) and to one another. In 3-D, the Cartesian coordinate system is defined by three mutually perpendicular planes, usually referred to as x, y, and z.

cathode-ray tube (CRT)

A video monitor based on cathode-ray tube technology. The CRT operates by firing an electron beam that strikes the inside of the monitor's display surface, which is coated with *phosphor*. The phosphor glows briefly when excited by the beam. Color CRTs have a shadow mask which the beam passes through on its way to the phosphor. The shadow mask ensures that the guns excite only phosphors of the color upon which they were fired.

central structure store (CSS)

The *PHIGS* display list structure. The CSS is an editable hierarchy of structures composed of: elements, attributes and *transformations*. CSS elements are drawing primitives such as lines and polygons and CSS *attributes* are qualities such as color and style. See also *hierarchical data structures*.

child structure

A data record in a hierarchical data structure. The *child structure* is said to be invoked by its *parent structure*, and it inherits its parent's *attributes*. This hierarchy is used by *PHIGS*.

client

In the client/server model for file systems, the client is a machine that remotely accesses resources of a compute server, such as compute power and large memory capacity. In the client/server model for window systems, the client is an *application* that accesses windowing services from a "server process." In this model, the client and the server can run on the same machine or on separate machines.

clipping

A 2-D or 3-D operation that reduces the number of drawing calculations the CPU makes by eliminating any *objects*, or portions of objects, outside the viewing area.

clipping plane

In 3-D graphics, a plane inside the *view volume* (parallel to the *x, y-plane*), beyond which the *view volume* is not calculated or rendered. The clipping plane is employed to constrain the amount of memory required by a drawing. Any *object*, or portion of an object, occurring beyond the *clipping plane* is discarded. Often, there is both a front clipping plane and a back clipping plane.

closed surface

A solid surface with no holes such that none of the interior is visible. See also *backfacing polygon*.

color lookup table (CLUT)

See *color map*.

color map

The color options in a graphics system, arranged by index number. Typically, the system has a default color map. The index of colors in the color map can be reallocated, however, depending on the application. There is one color map in the hardware (often called a *color lookup table*), but many color maps can be allocated in software and indexed as appropriate for separate *applications*. See also *indexed color*.

color map animation

An animation method in which the *object* or character does not actually move but is made to appear as if it is moving. The consecutive images are drawn on subsets of the *bit planes* in the *frame buffer* in a different stage of movement. All the bit planes are visible simultaneously; the color map is used to cycle through the animation sequence on the bit planes, illuminating just one of the duplicate images at a time in the object color and the remainder of the objects in the background color. This is an advantageous method, because it is faster to change the colors in the color map than it is to redraw the image again and again.

computer-aided design (CAD)

Use of computer graphics technology to design electronic and mechanical parts and machinery.

computer graphics

The processes associated with producing images by digital rendering of a picture model.

compute server

See *server*.

concave

Pertaining to a region or shape, such as a *polygon*, for which at least one straight line segment between two points of the region is not entirely contained within the region. See also *convex*.

control points

The points (in *model coordinates*) that control the shape of a curve or curved surface.

convex

Pertaining to a region or shape, such as a *polygon*, for which a straight line segment between any two points of the region is entirely contained within the region. Contrast with *concave*.

coordinate points

Points in a *Cartesian* system at which axes converge. Specific coordinates can be selected by referring to the numbered points along the axes of the particular *coordinate system*. For instance, the coordinates (3, 4) in a two-dimensional coordinate system denote a coordinate point that is 3 points to the right of the origin along the x-axis and 4 points up the y-axis. The coordinates (3, 4, 5) in a three-dimensional coordinate system denote a coordinate point that is 3 points along x, 4 points along y, and 5 points along z.

coordinate system

The particular mathematical system of axes in which points and lines can be plotted by virtue of their distance from the *origin*, or placed at various steps in the *viewing pipeline*. Locations where the x and y (2-D) or the x, y, and z (3-D) coordinates cross are called *coordinate points*.

CRT

See *cathode-ray tube*.

CSS

See *central structure store*.

DAC

See *digital-to-analog converter*.

damage to window images

Caused when one window is overlaid on top of another window and then moved or removed. Damage is repaired by the *window system* from saved pixel values, or by the *graphics library* from data stored in a display list.

depth buffer

See *Z-buffer*.

depth-cueing

In 3-D graphics, the process of reducing the intensity (in color or gray scale) of the lines or surfaces of an *object* as it recedes from the viewer. This fading technique helps establish visual order in objects that might otherwise appear confusing or flat, and it improves a scene's visual depth.

device coordinates

The coordinates in the *coordinate system* that describe the physical units by which the computer screen is defined.

device-dependent

Software that has been written for a specific computer device, and runs on that device exclusively. Software that can run only on a specific vendor's computer hardware is known as vendor-dependent.

An Introduction to Computer Graphics Concepts

device driver

The software that converts *device-independent* graphics commands into device-specific (*device-dependent*) display.

device-independent

Software that has been written expressly for portability across dissimilar computer systems. An *industry standard* graphics library, such as PHIGS, is a device-independent interface.

diffuse highlight

Object highlights that result when a light source interacts with a non-reflective surface.

digital image

An image that has been converted into an array of pixels. See also *digitization*.

digital-to-analog converter (DAC)

A mechanical or electronic device that is used to convert discrete digital numbers to continuous analog signals. Opposite of analog-to-digital converter. See also *digitize*.

digitize

To convert an image from hard copy (such as a photo) into digital (binary) data for display on a computer. Also, to convert an analog signal (voltage or temperature) into a digital value.

directional light

Light emanating from a light source that is virtually infinite (the light rays are essentially parallel) such as the sun. Contrast with *ambient light*.

display device

The hardware device that displays windows, text, icons, and graphical pictures. Typically, a display device is a *frame buffer* and monitor.

display list

A description of the desired image via a list of *primitives* and *attributes*. Display lists provide an intermediate picture storage for quick image redraw. In *GKS*, the display list is a 2-D, segmented data storage method and cannot be edited. In *PHIGS*, the display list structure is a 3-D, hierarchical data list that can be edited. See also *immediate mode*.

dithering

An increase in variations between a picture's colors or gray values reduces some spatial resolution quality, but gains patterns of pixel arrays. This technique is used when there are not enough bits in the frame buffer to represent true color.

double buffering

The process of using two *frame buffers* for smooth *animation*. Graphical contents of one frame buffer are displayed while updates occur on the other buffer. When the updates are complete, the buffers are switched. Only complete images are displayed, and the process of drawing is not shown. The result is the appearance of smooth animation.

edge

In graphics: one or more *vectors* defining a portion of an *object*. In *image processing*: a set of values determined (by an *edge-detection* algorithm) to be the dividing line between one image and another or an image and background color.

edge detection

An image-processing technique in which edge pixels are identified by examining their neighboring pixels.

edge enhancement

An image enhancement technique in which edges are sharpened by increasing the contrast between the lighter and darker pixels on opposite sides of the edge.

eight-bit color

The color range possible with an eight-bit graphics system. Each pixel in an 8-bit system can display one of 256 colors (2^8) at any given time. These colors are typically obtained from a *color map*. See also *indexed color*.

electron beam

The beam of electrons produced by the *electron gun*.

electron gun

The device within the computer CRT that produces an electron beam. The electron beam illuminates the *phosphors* of the monitor to display the *pixels* on the *raster* grid in a selected pattern.

extent

See *bounding box*.

eye point

The location of the eye in 3-D space. Like a camera, the eye is not statically confined to one location in an area defining a picture. The *eye point*, or camera, can be repositioned anywhere. In 3-D graphics, the user does not simply have a view of an environment from a confined area. Rather, the eye point location can go anywhere in the space. Thus, the images move, but the user's eye point can move dynamically in the space as well.

face

Faces are parts of *planes* that form an object surface, such as a polyhedron (cube or prism). As an example, a cube has six faces.

face list

The list of *faces* and their vertices that make up the surface shape of a *mesh model*.

facet

See *face*.

faceted shading

See *flat shading*.

fill algorithm

An *algorithm* that fills *polygons* with a color, gray-scale shade, or pattern.

filtering

An image-processing technique that reduces unwanted features or colors in an image.

flat shading

Also called *faceted shading*. A shading method that applies a *lighting model* to only one point on each polygon face. Each face is rendered in a single color that represents the amount of light interacting with that face. This tends to give the object a faceted look, like a diamond.

fractal

Short for "fractional dimensional." Fractal geometry uses "self-similarity" to create complex objects. Self-similarity is the result of recursive reproduction of an object so that each reproduction is similar (identical in geometry) to the original. An extremely complex image results from the composite of the infinite self-similar reproductions. Fractals are used in graphics for the creation of images such as coastlines, trees, and clouds.

frame buffer

Display memory that temporarily stores (buffers) a full frame of picture data at one time. Frame buffers are composed of arrays of *bit* values that correspond to the display's *pixels*. The number of bits per pixel in the frame buffer determines the complexity of images that can be displayed. See also *double buffering*.

gamma correction

The intensity of the luminescent phosphor on the raster display when struck by the electron beam is non-linear. Gamma correction is an adjustment to the color map to make up for this inherent nonlinearity, and results in a truer mix of colors when objects are displayed.

geographic information systems (GIS)

A graphics application using a database of specialized information, such as geographical and demographic data. Applications written for the GIS market use the database information to determine such things as the best location for a new fire station or shopping center, the most likely location of archeological remains, and so on.

geographic mapping

An application for graphics systems used for a variety of projects such as city planning. These applications usually rely on large databases of information that can be used to provide meaningful mapping information, such as street names, zip codes, and census data. See also *geographic information systems*.

GIS

See *geographic information systems*.

GKS

The Graphical Kernel System. An international standard 2-D *graphics library* consisting of a set of defined graphic *primitive*s and a tool set for application programmers. GKS is designed to free the programmer of many of the low-level programming tasks involved in creating and manipulating graphics on a workstation. Applications written with GKS can run in *immediate mode, display list*, or both.

Gouraud shading

(Rhymes with Thoreau.) A sophisticated shading method capable of producing realistic results. This method applies a *lighting model* to each vertex of a polygon face, and *interpolates* the results across the face to achieve a smooth lighting effect.

An Introduction to Computer Graphics Concepts

graphic primitive

See *primitive*.

graphical user interface (GUI)

The graphical user interface, or GUI, provides the user with a method of interacting with the computer and its special applications, usually via a mouse or another selection device. The GUI usually includes such things as windows, an intuitive method of manipulating directories and files, and *icons*.

graphics accelerator

A hardware device dedicated to increasing the speed and performance of graphics. Graphics accelerators calculate pixel values, and write them into the *frame buffer*, freeing up the CPU for other operations.

graphics library

A tool set for application programmers, interfaced with an *application programmer's interface*, or API. The graphics library usually includes a defined set of *primitives* and function calls that enable the programmer to bypass many low-level programming tasks.

graphics routine

A collection of code in a computer program that draws graphical objects.

gray-scale manipulation

An image enhancement technique in which the appearance of a *digital image* is improved by adjusting its gray levels.

GUI

See *graphical user interface*.

hardware

The components of a computer graphics system responsible for user input, display, and mathematical processing. Often the term hardware is used in specific reference to the computing power of the CPU or the *graphics accelerator*, or both. Another term for the collection of compute hardware is *platform*.

hidden line removal

In three-dimensional wireframe graphics, an algorithm that eliminates the lines from a drawing that would be hidden if the *object* were opaque. This method reduces the potential of ambiguity in an object's appearance.

hidden surface removal

An *algorithm* that ensures that *object* surfaces which are closer to the viewer in *three-dimensional* space are drawn so that they *occlude* any objects or portions of objects that should be hidden behind them. See also *Z-buffer*.

hierarchical data structures

In *PHIGS*, a system that defines *objects* in hierarchical relationship to one another. The hierarchical data organization enables structures (descendants) to inherit the *attributes* of other structures (ancestors), which enables the programmer to manipulate objects efficiently.

high-level software

Generally refers to software that is not operationally close to the hardware. Graphical user interfaces, for instance, are high level because they pass through a pipeline that includes the window system software, and they do not "talk" directly to the hardware. By contrast, *low-level* software does talk directly to the hardware.

highlight

The result of *directional* light sources cast upon an object surface. See also *specular highlight*. Also: to change the intensity or color of an *object* or *primitive* to make it more noticeable.

icon

A tiny on-screen symbol that simplifies access to a program, command, or data file. Many workstations in a networking environment, for instance, use a mailbox icon to symbolize an electronic mail-reading utility. The mailbox is activated by moving the mouse pointer onto the icon and pressing a button or key.

image enhancement

The process of improving the appearance of an image using techniques such as edge enhancement, gray-scale manipulation, *smoothing*, and *sharpening*.

image processing

One of the methods used to enhance or manipulate the characteristics of a scanned or digitized image for analysis. Typical image-processing techniques include *filtering* and *thresholding*.

image reconstruction

An imaging technology used in a variety of industries, including *medical imaging*. Image data are gathered through one of several methods, including CAT-scan and magnetic resonance imaging. These data are processed (reconstructed) into viewable 2-D or 3-D images. See also *slices*.

image restoration

The process of returning an image to its original condition by reversing the effects of degradations.

imaging

The broad category of image-related computer technologies that includes *computer graphics*, *image processing*, *image reconstruction*, and *scientific visualization*.

immediate mode

A method for handling graphical data where the *graphics library* does not retain any copy of the data belonging to the picture on the graphics display. The application is responsible for storing (or regenerating) the data, in contrast to the *display list* method, in which the graphics library retains its own copy of the graphical data.

indexed color

Also *pseudo-color*. Indexed color graphics systems are usually equipped with from 8 to 12 memory bits per pixel. A limited set of colors, selected from a much larger color palette, are indexed in a color lookup table or *color map*, and the *application* accesses them by their index numbers.

industry standard

Elements of a computer system hardware or software subsystem that have been standardized and adopted by the industry at large. Standardization occurs in two ways: through a rigorous procedure followed by the *ANSI* and *ISO* organizations, or through wide acceptance by the industry. Standards enable users, such as application developers, to write software applications using a standard set of tools.

input device

A hardware device that enables the user to communicate with the graphics system. Examples of input devices are keyboard, mouse, track ball, light pen, and joystick.

International Standards Organization (ISO)

An international agency that reviews and approves independently designed products for use within specific industries. ISO is also responsible for developing standards for information exchange. Its function is similar to that of *ANSI* in the United States.

interpolation

A method of determining intermediate values between those provided, such as shades of pink along a line (or across a *polygon*) between *vertex* colors of white and red. See also *depth-cueing* and *shading*.

ISO

See *International Standards Organization*.

jaggies

A term for the jagged visual appearance of lines and shapes in raster pictures that results from producing graphics on a grid format. This effect can be reduced by increasing the *sample rate* in *scan conversion*. See also *antialiasing*.

knots

Scalar values—in addition to the *control points*—that influence a curve shape. They may be non-uniformly spaced in *NURBS*.

LAN

See *local area network*.

lighting model

A mathematical formula for approximating the physical effect of light from various sources striking *objects*. Typical lighting models use light sources, and the object's position, orientation (that is, the orientation of its *surface normals*), and surface type (such as color and shininess). See also *shading method*.

light pen

A light detection device used for graphical input. The user points the light pen at a location on the graphics display. When the *electron gun* illuminates the *phosphor*, the light pen detects the light and sends a signal to the workstation, which records the *pixel* event at that moment.

light source

One of several types of light used by a *lighting model*. Light source types include *ambient*, *directional*, positional, and spot. The last two types are called local light sources.

An Introduction to Computer Graphics Concepts

local area network (LAN)

A group of computer systems in close proximity that can communicate with one another via some connecting hardware and software.

lookup table

See *color map*.

low level software

Generally refers to software that "talks" directly to the processing hardware. Programming with low level software gives the programmer more control, but it also requires special expertise, and tends to be more time consuming than working with high-level software such as *graphics library* standards.

LUT

An abbreviation for lookup table. See *color map*.

magnetic resonance imaging (MRI)

A medical imaging technique that is used for image capture. Tissue area is simultaneously subjected to electromagnetic radiation and a magnetic field. Sample data slices are gathered and are later reconstructed into a composite image for further processing and analysis.

mapping

The transformation of one coordinate system into another. In the 3-D *viewing pipeline*, for instance, an *object* is defined by the application developer in *model coordinates*; these are mapped to *world coordinates*; the world coordinates are mapped to *normalized device coordinates* (NDCs); the NDCs are mapped into *device coordinates*; and the final picture is displayed. Also, an application for computer graphics systems. See *geographic mapping*, and *geographic information systems*.

marker

See *polymarker*.

MCAD

Mechanical computer-aided design. A specialized computer graphics market for the design of mechanical structures, such as automobiles, airplanes, and their parts.

medical imaging

A field that employs various image-generation techniques, such as computed axial tomography (CAT-scan), magnetic resonance imaging (MRI), and X-ray to collect image samples from a patient's internal tissue for analysis.

megabyte

A megabyte is 1,048,576 bytes or 1024 kilobytes; or roughly 1 million bytes or 1,000 kilobytes.

mesh model

A graphical model with a mesh surface constructed from *polygons* (specifically *quadrilaterals*, if the polygons are four-sided). The polygons in a mesh are described by the graphics system as solid faces, rather than as hollow polygons, as is the case with *wireframe models*. Separate portions of mesh that make up the mesh model are called *polygon mesh* and *quadrilateral mesh*.

MFLOPS

An acronym for millions of floating point operations per second. MFLOPS are standardized units of execution speed used to rate the floating point performance of a computer.

MIPS

An acronym for *millions of instructions per second*. MIPS are standardized units of execution speed used to rate the performance of a computer *CPU*.

model coordinates

The coordinate system used for describing a single *object*. When each object is described in its own model coordinate space, all are mapped to one *world coordinate* space.

modeling

The method of creating an *object* in computer graphics through computational descriptions of the object's polygonal makeup, surface shape, and *attributes*.

molecular modeling

A sophisticated chemical engineering application using computer graphics to simulate chemical reactions in molecules.

mouse

An input device connected to the workstation that determines the location of the *pointer* and thus determines the active window in a *window system*. The user manipulates the position of the mouse next to the workstation, causing an update to occur in the position of the pointer on the display.

MRI

See *magnetic resonance imaging*.

multi-bit raster

A raster that has more than one *bit plane*. The number of colors or gray-scale values that can be contained in the raster increases exponentially with an increase in the number of bits per pixel assigned to the raster. An 8-bit raster can hold 256 colors or gray-scale values, and a 24-bit raster can hold over 16 million values.

multimarker

See *polymarker.*

NDC

See *normalized device coordinates.*

noise

Irrelevant data that hamper the recognition and interpretation of the data of interest.

Non-Uniform Rational B-Spline (NURBS)

A curve definition method based on the *B-spline*, which offers additional flexibility via *knots* along the spline. Some knots can be given more weight (sort of like a magnet) than others to pull the curve toward those knots. This feature enables the user to create 2-D curves and 3-D surfaces generalized from those curves with precision.

normal

Adjective: perpendicular or *orthogonal*. At right angles to another line segment, *object*, or *plane*. Noun: a *surface normal*. The *vector* that is perpendicular to a surface at a specific point.

normal vector

A vector that is perpendicular (or *orthogonal*) to a surface or plane at a specific point.

normalized device coordinates (NDCs)

The coordinate system between the user's *world coordinates* and the graphics system's physical *device coordinates* in the *viewing pipeline*. For each axis in the coordinate system, the normalized device coordinates are typically sized so that objects within that coordinate system range from -1.0 to 1.0.

NURBS

See *Non-Uniform Rational B-Spline.*

object

A graphics entity. A single image or *model* defined in 2-D or 3-D space.

occlusion

The result of an object or a portion of an object surface being drawn behind another solid object or opaque surface. An occluded object or window is one that is hidden from view.

origin

The location in *Cartesian coordinates* from which the axes that define 2-D and 3-D space originate. This is the location (0, 0) in 2-D graphics and (0, 0, 0) in 3-D graphics. The positions of graphical objects can be described in absolute terms, relative to the origin.

orthogonal

Perpendicular, or *normal*.

output primitive

Simple graphical objects provided by a graphics library for use in the construction of more complex objects. Output primitives in *GKS* include polyline, polymarker, text, fill area, cell array, and generalized drawing primitive (GDP). Output primitives in *PHIGS* include polyline, polymarker, text, fill area, fill area set, cell array, and GDP. *PHIGS PLUS* adds more sophisticated primitives, such as *quadrilateral mesh* and *NURBS* curves and surfaces.

overlay

A graphics image superimposed over a portion of another image. An example of this is when one window partially *occludes* another window.

overlay planes

Bit planes in the *frame buffer* can be assigned as overlay planes to enable images to be superimposed over one another. Images in the overlay planes can be superimposed over the frame buffer image without causing *damage* to the image in the frame buffer. The application is therefore not required to redraw the picture in the frame buffer when it is overlaid by other windows. This is especially beneficial when the data in the rest of the *frame buffer* are extremely complex.

parallel projection

The process of projecting an image from the 3-D *view volume* onto the 2-D graphics display with parallel projectors. Objects at any distance from the *eye point* maintain their apparent size under parallel projection. These projectors are *orthogonal* to the 2-D plane. See also *perspective projection*.

parent structure

The first of two or more connected objects in a *hierarchical data structure* system, such as *PHIGS*. A parent structure invokes its *child structure*, which inherits the parent's *attributes*.

particle systems

A method of graphically producing the appearance of amorphous substances, such as clouds, smoke, and fire. The substance is described as a collection of particles that can be manipulated dynamically for animation effects.

patch

A portion of an *object* surface defined by some number of points. Patches are separately defined and then pieced together to form the skin of an object, like a patchwork quilt. Surface patches can either be *planar* (flat) or curved.

pattern recognition

In *image processing*, the analysis, description, identification, and classification of objects or other meaningful regularities.

perspective projection

The process of projecting an image from the 3-D *view volume* to the 2-D graphics display with projector lines that converge at the *eye point*. Objects appear to get smaller if they are further from the eye point.

PEX

The PHIGS Extension to X; a protocol for 3-D graphics in a network window system that supports both *PHIGS* and *PHIGS PLUS* features.

PHIGS

The Programmer's Hierarchical Interactive Graphics System. An international standard 3-D graphics library consisting of a graphical tool set for *application programmers*. *PHIGS* uses hierarchical data structures. Objects can be created, altered, manipulated, and stored by the user, dynamically. PHIGS is designed for easy portability to many graphics systems.

PHIGS PLUS

Programmer's Hierarchical Interactive Graphics System *Plus Lumière Und Surfaces*. An extension to *PHIGS* that includes additional capabilities, such as lighting from single and multiple sources, *depth-cueing*, *NURBS*, and complex geometric *primitives*. PHIGS PLUS is a proposed standard, currently under review.

PHIGS structures

See *hierarchical data structures.*

Phong shading

A sophisticated shading method, developed by Phong Bui-tuong. By calculating the light at many points across an object surface, Phong shading produces highly realistic effects and more accurate *specular highlights* than *Gouraud shading.*

phosphor

A luminescent substance on the inside of the *cathode-ray tube* display that is illuminated by the *electron gun* in the pattern of graphical images as the display is scanned.

picking

A feature of a *graphics library* that enables an application user to select primitives and objects with a pointing device.

pixel

Short for picture element. In a *raster* grid, the pixel is the smallest unit that can be addressed and given a color or intensity. The pixel is represented by some number of *bits* in the *frame buffer,* and is illuminated by a collection of *phosphor* dots in the *CRT* that are struck by the beam(s) of the *electron gun.*

pixmap

The array of values in the *frame buffer* for a given picture, particularly in the case of multi-bit displays. See also *bitmap.*

planar

Lying on one *plane.* Planar primitives, such as triangles, have all of their vertices on a single plane, which makes it a simple matter to calculate the orientation of the primitive, as well as the orientation of the *surface normal,* used in the calculation of light on the surface. *Quadrilaterals,* by contrast, may or may not be planar.

plane

An infinite space defined by any three points that do not lie in the same straight line. To picture this, draw a triangle on a piece of paper. Pick up the paper and position it anywhere in the space around you. Imagine that the triangle defines a plane that stretches into infinity in all directions. Moving the paper to a new position defines a new plane. (Note that the piece of paper is on the same plane; the three points of the triangle are the minimum number of points that can define a plane.)

platform

The compute hardware in the graphics system (or other computer). *Applications* are often designed with the support of a particular platform from a particular vendor in mind.

pointer

In a *window system*, the arrow or other marker that indicates to the window system and to the user which window is active. The user positions the pointer within a chosen window. The pointer is also called a cursor, although the term cursor should be reserved for the text marker that indicates the current input location for a text character.

polygon

A *planar* shape created by a set of connected line segments (or *vectors*) that form *vertices* at their meeting points. Note that an n-gon is a polygon with an undetermined number of sides.

polygon mesh

A portion of a *mesh model* surface constructed from *polygons* (usually *quadrilaterals*).

polyline

A set of coordinate points connected by a set of line segments, defined in *GKS* as an *output primitive*. The set of points is contained in an array or list of points.

polymarker

In *GKS* and *PHIGS*, a set of points defined as an *output primitive*. These primitives appear as small symbols, and are often used in graphs and charts. Common marker types are crosses, circles, squares, and dots.

primitive

Fundamental shapes and objects in computer graphics, used primarily in construction of more complex objects. Graphics primitives include point, line segment, polyline, circle, ellipse, triangle, square, and rectangle.

processor

A hardware device that executes the commands in a stored program in the computer system. In addition to the *central processing unit*, many sophisticated graphics systems contain a dedicated processor for *graphics acceleration*.

projection

The process of reducing the dimension of a 3-D image for display on the 2-D graphics display. There are several methods, among them *parallel projection* and *perspective projection*.

pseudo-color

See *indexed color*.

quad

An abbreviation for *quadrilateral*.

quadrilateral

A closed polygon with four vertices, and thus four sides. Quadrilaterals, or quads, can be *planar*, in which case all vertices lie on the same plane, or non-planar. With non-planar quadrilaterals (sometimes called bow ties, because of their shape), it is more difficult to calculate orientation and lighting, and thus many systems *tessellate* quads to triangles, which are definitively planar.

quadrilateral mesh

A surface defined by four-sided polygons, each attached to other quadrilaterals. See *mesh model*.

quantization

In *image processing*, a process in which each *pixel* in an image is assigned one of a finite set of gray levels.

radiosity

A technique that calculates the lighting in a complex diffuse lighting environment, based on the geometry of the scene. Results are highly realistic. Because the radiosity calculations do not take into account the eye point of the viewer, the geometry and lighting in the environment do not need to be recalculated if the eye point changes. This makes it possible to produce many scenes that are part of the same environment (the rooms in a building, for instance), and to "walk through" the environment in real time. See also *ray tracing*.

raster

A rectangular grid of picture elements, or *pixels*. The graphical data to be displayed on the raster is stored by the frame buffer. Raster operations (or *raster ops*) can be performed on some portion or all of the raster. Such operations aid in the efficient handling of blocks of pixel data. For instance, *bit blts* move blocks of bits from one portion of the *frame buffer* to another.

raster ops

Logical operations (known as ANDs, ORs, NORs, etc.) performed on portions of the *bit planes*—known as *bitmaps* or *pixmaps*—in the *frame buffer*. These operations are used to perform fundamental movements and transfers of pixel data. See *bit blt*.

raster scan

A display device technology in which raster data are scanned onto the monitor by an electron beam that sweeps constantly across the surface. Also, the process of methodically scanning the *raster* (the contents of the *frame buffer*), and using the values to control the intensity of the *electron beam*.

ray tracing

An advanced method of determining light interaction, such as reflection and refraction, in a graphical lighting environment. Rays are traced from the light source to the *eye point*, or from the eye point to the light source, to determine what the eye sees through each *pixel* on the display. Ray tracing tends to yield realistic results, but it is computationally expensive. See also *radiosity*.

real time

The accelerated graphics processing that makes objects appear to move naturally and at a speed that appears realistic. Also, the visual result of some combination of effective *transformation* algorithms, fine-tuning of the graphics software to the graphics hardware, *double-buffering*, and graphics *acceleration*.

refresh rate

The rate at which successive frames of a raster display are swept by the scanning beam.

relative coordinates

Coordinates relative to a coordinate system whose origin is set at the initial position of a point selected on an object. This new coordinate system represents a *transformation* relative to the origin in *absolute coordinates*. Relative coordinates provide the application with the flexibility to wait until the last minute for final placement of an object in *device coordinates*. At that time, the location of the initial coordinate is established, and the remaining object coordinates fall into place with respect to that coordinate.

remote sensing

A method of gathering image data remotely, such as by aerial photography or satellite.

rendering

The process of computing a graphical model's surface qualities, such as color, *shading*, smoothness, and texture, and creating a raster image.

resolution

The number of *pixels* in the horizontal and vertical dimensions of a display, taking into account the size of the display, and thus the size of the pixels. Also, the number of elements per unit length available for display or printing by a particular device. For instance, 1200 dots per inch is considered to be excellent print resolution.

RGB color

RGB color systems obtain their colors via a direct combination of red, green, and blue components. The range of colors that can be displayed depends upon the number of bits that have been assigned to each *pixel*. See also *true color*.

rotation

A geometric *transformation* that causes a graphical object to revolve around a point (in 2-D) or around an axis (in 3-D).

sample rate

The frequency of the points used to determine an object's placement on the display device. See *sampling*.

sampling

A procedure that samples many points across an object's lines or surfaces to determine its placement in pixels. This occurs during *scan conversion*.

scaling

A geometric *transformation* that causes an object to be increased or decreased in size.

scan conversion

The process of converting picture data in digital form to pixel data in analog (voltage) form.

scan line

The parallel lines that are defined by the scan of the *electron beam* inside the CRT. Also, one line of *pixels* in the *frame buffer* corresponding to the above.

scanner

A hardware device that converts a hard copy image, such as a photograph, into digital data for display on a graphics system.

scientific visualization

Technology that enables scientists to store vast amounts of mathematical data, generate graphical models that represent the data, and visually analyze the results, usually through interactive software programs.

screen coordinates

See *device coordinates*.

screen space

The space defined by pixel coordinates. See also *device coordinates*.

segment

A portion of a *primitive* or picture, such as a line segment. In the *GKS graphics library*, a collection of picture data composed of primitives and *attributes*. See also *structure*.

shading

The *interpolation* of color across objects, typically after lighting.

shading method

A technique for creating graphical realism by applying the *lighting model* at points on the *object primitives*. The result is the identification of appropriate colors for the object's pixels. See also *interpolation, flat shading, Gouraud shading,* and *Phong shading*.

shadow mask

A metal plate with tiny holes carefully positioned inside the *CRT* hardware. The electron beam passes from the *electron gun*, through a hole in the shadow mask, which guides the beam and ensures its precise placement on the inside of the display surface. The mask ensures that electrons from the "red gun" hit the red phosphor, that electrons from the "green gun" hit the green phosphor, and that the electrons from the "blue gun" hit the blue phosphor.

sharpening

Any image enhancement technique in which the effect of blurring in the original image is reduced.

server

In the client/server model for file systems, the server is a machine with compute resources (and is sometimes called the compute server), and large memory capacity. Client machines can remotely access and make use of these resources. In the client/server model for window systems, the server is a process that provides windowing services to an application, or "client process." In this model, the client and the server can run on the same machine or on separate machines.

SIGGRAPH

The Special Interest Group for Graphics, sponsored by the Association for Computing Machinery. SIGGRAPH sponsors an annual conference on graphics that includes many vendor product displays, lectures by professionals in the field, and courses on graphics technology.

slices

Sample 2-D data arrays gathered through one of several methods, such as CAT-scan and magnetic resonance imaging, for 3-D *image reconstruction*.

smoothing

Any image enhancement technique in which the effect of *noise* in the original image is reduced.

smooth shading

A shading method, such as *Gouraud* or *Phong shading*, that blends colors smoothly across the object.

solid model

See *surface model*.

solids modeling

The creation and rendering of graphical models as solids with properties such as mass and weight.

specular highlight

Light reflected from a shiny surface. Typically, a specular highlight appears as a small but intense reflection on an object surface. Metallic objects have specular reflections in bright light. The *Phong* shading method is most accurate in producing this effect.

spline curves

See *B-splines* and *NURBS*.

staircasing

The visual stair step effect that results from drawing pictures on a grid (raster). See also *aliasing* and *jaggies*.

structure

In *PHIGS*, a sequence of *structure elements* describing graphical objects, and possibly invoking other structures in a hierarchical fashion.

structure element

In *PHIGS*, structure elements are the graphical data (such as *output primitives* and their *attributes*) that are used to create graphical objects. See also *hierarchical data structures*.

surface model

A model constructed of polygons. These can be hollow (giving the model an appearance similar to that of a *wireframe model*) or solid-filled. The surface model is often called a solid model, although this term can be misleading.

surface normal

The vector that is perpendicular to a point on an object's surface or plane. A surface normal can be used to calculate light on the object surface.

tablet

A hardware device used in conjunction with a pen-like stylus or mouse-like puck to *digitize* an image for graphical display.

tessellate

To divide a curve or surface into geometric forms to calculate their shapes and dimensions for simplified processing and rendering. Many systems tessellate *quadrilaterals*, which are not always *planar*, into triangles, which are definitively planar.

texture mapping

The process of superimposing a 2-D texture or pattern over the surface of a 3-D graphical object. This is an efficient method for producing the appearance of texture, such as that of wood or stone, on a large surface area.

three-dimensional graphics

The display of objects and scenes with height, width, and depth information. The information is calculated in a coordinate system that represents three dimensions via x, y, and z axes. Also expressed as 3-D.

threshold

In *image processing*, a specified gray level used for producing a binary image. See also *thresholding*.

thresholding

The process of producing greater contrast in a gray-scale image by assigning each *pixel* the value 1 if the image portion it represents is at or above a specified gray level (the *threshold*) and the value 0 if the image portion is below that threshold. The result is a high-contrast black and white image that highlights certain features.

tile

To cover a surface with non-overlapping polygons or other geometric objects.

transformation

A change made in an object's size, location, or orientation. Transformations include *scaling, translation*, and *rotation*. Also, "transform."

translation

Movement of an object along the x-, y-, and/or z-axes.

traversal

The process of reading a *display list* and passing on the graphics information to the *viewing pipeline*.

true color

Also known as *RGB color* or 24-bit color. True color graphics systems are usually equipped with at least 24 bits per pixel. In the 24-bit system, for instance, three primary colors in the color graphics system—red, green and blue—are allotted 8 bits each. There are 2^8, or 256 intensities each for red, green, and blue. This translates to a total palette range of 16.7 million colors (256 x 256 x 256). Because the human eye cannot detect the subtlety available in a palette of 16.7 million colors, this range makes it possible to compute what appears to be gradual *shading*.

twenty-four-bit color

See *true color.*

two-dimensional graphics

Graphics displayed in two dimensions: height and width. The two-dimensional display is represented by two axes, x (horizontal) and y (vertical). The surface spanning the parameters of the horizontal and vertical axes is called the *x, y-plane*. Also expressed as 2-D.

user interface

See *graphical user interface.*

An Introduction to Computer Graphics Concepts

vector

A line segment on a display surface, especially one that is of minimum width and solid (no dashing). A vector can also be a conceptual direction (perhaps with length) denoting a direction (of a light ray, for instance) or the boundary of an object; an example is a *normal vector*.

vertex

The location at which vectors and polygon faces or edges intersect. The vertices of an object are used in transformation algorithms to describe the object's location and its location in relation to other objects.

viewing pipeline

The process by which picture data are translated from user input to the screen display. In the 3-D viewing pipeline, for instance, an object is defined by the application developer in *model coordinates*; the model coordinates are mapped to *world coordinates*; the world coordinates are mapped to *normalized device coordinates* (NDCs); the NDCs are mapped into *device coordinates*; and the final picture is displayed.

view volume

In 3-D graphics, the conceptual 3-D space between the user's eye point and infinity. The depth of the view volume becomes finite if front and back *clipping planes* are used to limit the drawing space available to the application. The width of the view volume, though theoretically infinite, is limited by the edges of the display surface.

visualization

One of a number of methods used to create graphical models to represent complex (typically scientific) data. See also *volume rendering* and *medical imaging*.

volume rendering

A method of computing solid volume data for graphical display in volumetric models composed of 3-D elements called *voxels*. Direct volume-rendering techniques enable the user to manipulate the volume data as a solid structure that can be sliced open to expose internal views.

voxel

Short for volume element, the word voxel is an adaptation of the word *pixel*. Voxels are three-dimensional elements that describe the data in a volumetric structure. See also *volume rendering*.

window system

A system that provides the user with a multi-use environment on the display device. Separate windows are like separate displays on the monitor screen. Each window can run its own application. The user brings up some number of windows for various applications, and the window system handles the communications between each of the applications and the hardware.

wireframe model

An object with edges created by line segments. Because the object is wholly transparent, the object's *hidden lines* are visible (unless an algorithm is employed to remove them). The advantage is the efficiency with which such an object can be drawn since no surfaces need to be rendered or highlighted. Wireframe models can be drawn much more quickly than *surface models*. The disadvantage is that in a complex 3-D drawing (a car engine, for example), it may be difficult for the viewer to make visual sense of the drawing. See also *depth-cueing* and *hidden line removal*.

world coordinates

The coordinate system that is scaled so that user-defined objects can be represented in units appropriate to the application, such as inches, meters, and miles. Each object in a picture is first described in its own *model coordinates*, and all are then mapped into world coordinates.

x-axis

The horizontal axis in the *Cartesian coordinate system*. Although coordinate systems can be moved and their orientations altered, the x-axis is always perpendicular to the *y-axis*.

Xlib

An *API (application programmer's interface)* that gives application programmers access to the routines of the *X Window System*. These routines control display, event management, input and output.

X Window System

A window system developed by a group of engineers at the Massachusetts Institute of Technology. Its most prominent feature is its protocol for communications across a computer network. It has become a de facto standard through wide adoption in the computer industry. See also *PEX*.

x, y-plane

The plane that is created by the x and y axes in a *coordinate system*.

y-axis

The vertical axis in the *Cartesian coordinate system*. Although coordinate systems can be moved, and their orientations altered, the y-axis is always perpendicular to the x-axis.

z-axis

The axis, in 3-D graphics, representing depth. The z-axis runs perpendicular to the x, *y-plane*, and when added to the *x-axis* (width information) and the *y-axis* (height information), the z-axis forms a virtual three-dimensional space.

Z-buffer

The depth buffer in 3-D graphics. The Z-buffer memory locations, like those in the *frame buffer*, correspond to the *pixels* on the screen. The Z-buffer, however, contains information relating only to the *z-axis* (or depth axis). The Z-buffer is used in hidden surface removal algorithms, so that for each pixel written, the depth of that pixel is stored in the Z-buffer. When subsequent objects attempt to draw to that pixel, that object's z value is compared with the number in the Z-buffer, and the write is omitted if the object is farther away from the eye.

z clipping

Clipping of a three-dimensional object in the depth dimension in 3-D graphics.

Bibliography

Books

Burger, Peter and Gillies, Duncan. *Interactive Computer Graphics* London: Addison-Wesley, 1989.

Demel, John T. and Miller, Michael J. *Introduction to Computer Graphics* Belmont: Wadsworth, Inc., 1985.

Farin, Gerald *Curves and Surfaces for Computer Aided Geometric Design* San Diego: Academic Press, Inc., 1988.

Foley, James D.; van Dam, Andries; Feiner, Steve K.; Hughes, John F. *Computer Graphics: Principles and Practice, 2nd ed.* Reading, MA: Addison-Wesley, 1990.

Glassner, Andrew S., Editor *Graphics Gems* San Diego: Academic Press, Inc., 1990.

Gosling, James; Rosenthal, David S. H.; Arden, Michelle *The NeWS Book* New York: Springer-Verlag, 1989.

Hearn, Donald; Baker, Pauline M. *Computer Graphics* Englewood Cliffs, NJ: Prentice Hall, 1986.

Hill, Francis S. *Computer Graphics* New York: Macmillan, 1990.

Jain, Anil K. *Fundamentals of Digital Image Processing* Englewood Cliffs, NJ: Prentice Hall, 1989.

Pratt, William *Digital Image Processing* New York: Wiley Interscience, 1991.

Rogers, David F. *Procedural Elements for Computer Graphics* New York: McGraw-Hill, Inc., 1985.

Vince, John *The Language of Computer Graphics* New York: Van Nostrand Reinhold, 1990.

Winsor, Janice *OPEN LOOK Graphical User Interface Application Style Guidelines* Menlo Park: Addison-Wesley, 1990.

Winsor, Janice *OPEN LOOK Graphical User Interface Functional Specification* Menlo Park: Addison-Wesley, 1990.

Articles

Allen, William "Supercomputers Warming Up to Improve Greenhouse Models" *Supercomputing Review*, September 1989. pp. 26-30.

Brackett, Art "Small Town Firm Battles with CADD" *Design Management*, June 1990. pp. 10-13.

Brinkmann, Ron M. "3-D Graphics, From Alpha to Z-Buffer" *Byte*, July 1990. pp. 271-278.

Evans, Dave "Maps for Many Users" *Computer-Aided Engineering*, July 1989. pp. 104-106.

Glassner, Andrew S. "Ray Tracing for Realism" *Byte*, December 1990. pp. 263-271.

Killman, Peg and Kiely, Tom "Diagnostic Imaging Breaks the 2D Barrier" *Computer Graphics World*, August 1989. pp. 49-52.

McMillan, Donna; Johnson, Ruth; Mosher, Chuck "Volume Rendering on the TAAC-1" *SunTech Journal*, Autumn 1989. pp. 52-58.

Shoor, Rita "Targeting Treatment" *Computer Graphics World*, February 1990. pp. 38-46.

Smith, Alan D. "The Next Wave in Network Productivity" *Design Management*, June 1990. pp. 22-24.

Sorensen, Peter "Hair-Raising Graphics" *Computer Graphics World*, January 1990. pp. 45-48.

Thompson, John M. "Advanced Scientific Visualization Methods" *SunTech Journal*, July/August 1990. pp. 76-86.

Van Den Hoogen, Ingrid "Visual Design: Programming with SunPHIGS" *SunTech Journal*, Autumn 1989. pp. 63-73.

Wright, Jeff "Altered States" *Computer Graphics World*, December 1989. pp. 77-83.

Zenner Billet, Audrey "Measuring Graphics Performance" *SunTech Journal*, July/August 1990. pp. 36-46.

Technical Papers

Schechter, Greg; Stanton, W. Dean; Van Den Hoogen, Ingrid "PHIGS/GKS Technical White Paper" Sun Microsystems, Inc. June 1989.

Zenner Billet, Audrey "Graphics Performance Technical White Paper" Sun Microsystems, Inc. January 1990.

Index

C

CAD (computer-aided design), 143
California Institute of Technology, 95
Casteljau, Pierre, 76
cathode-ray tube (CRT), 10
CAT-scan (computed axial tomography), 127, 139
central processing unit (CPU), 13
central structure store (CSS), 121
chemical engineering, 149
child structures, 116
client
    file system, 26
    window system, 27
clipping
    2-D, 107
    3-D, 110
    plane, 110
    trivial accept, 108
    trivial reject, 108
CMY (cyan, magenta, yellow), 25
color, 41
    additive, 10, 25
    CMY (cyan, magenta, yellow), 25
    complement, 25, 37
    cube, 35
    indexed, 38 to 40
    mixing with the electron gun, 11
    primaries, 10
    pseudo, 38
    RGB (red, green, blue), 25
    subtractive, 25
color map, 38 to 40
computed tomography, 127
computer graphics
    and visual realism, 89
    computing, 13
    in real time, 90
    on networks, 26
computer-aided design (CAD), 143
computing lighting, 85
constant shading, 87

control points, 76
control polygons, 81
coordinate systems
    introduction, 32
    2-D, 51
    3-D, 33
    in viewing pipeline, 105
    synthetic camera, 54
coordinates
    2-D, 51
    device, 108
    model, 105 to 107
    normalized device (NDC), 108
    RGB (red, green, blue), 34
    world, 106 to 107
CPU (central processing unit), 13, 151
CRT (cathode-ray tube), 10
CSS (central structure store), 121
CT (computed tomography), 127
cursor, 16
curve fitting, 76
curved surface, 79, 82, 86
curves
    Bezier, 76
    B-spline, 78
    high-order, 76
    low-order, 76
    NURBS (Non-Uniform Rational B-Splines), 78 to 79
    smooth, 77

D

damage of pictures, 43, 119
Data General Corp., 123
data tablet, 23
DEC (Digital Equipment Corporation), 123
decreasing size (scaling), 103
depth clipping, 110
depth-cueing, 55
desktop publishing, 142
device coordinates, 108

An Introduction to Computer Graphics Concepts

An Introduction to Computer Graphics Concepts

RGB (red, green, blue)
  color cube, 35
  color model, 10, 25
  compared with CMY (cyan, magenta,
      yellow), 25
  coordinates, 34
  in color map, 40
  triple, 35
robot, 116
rotation, 104
  2-D, 104
  3-D, 105
rotational sweep, 82
run-time library, 20

S

sampling, 12, 59
scaling (zooming), 103
scan-conversion, 12, 25
scanners, 24
scene, 49
scientific visualization, 78, 133
segments, 120
server
  file system, 26
  window system, 27
shading, 85
  flat, 87
  Gouraud, 88
  Phong, 88
  smooth, 88
shooting
  in radiosity, 94
SIGGRAPH (Special Interest Group on
    Computer Graphics), 157
simulation, 134
  and analysis, 135
  fluid flows, 134
  molecular modeling, 149
sliders, 17
smooth shading, 88
software

application, 9, 18
  graphics library, 18
  interaction with hardware, 20
  window system, 14
Solbourne Computer Inc., 123
solid surface, 64, 68
Sony Corp., 123
Special Interest Group on Computer
    Graphics (SIGGRAPH), 157
SpectraGraphics, 123
specular highlights, 86, 88
stand-alone, 9
standards
  GKS (Graphical Kernel System), 120
  PEX (PHIGS Extension to X), 124
  PHIGS (Programmer's Hierarchical
      Interactive Graphics
      System), 121
  PHIGS PLUS, 121
  X Window System, 122
Stardent Computer Inc., 123
structures, 116
stylus, 23
subtractive colors, 25
Sun Microsystems Inc., 123
surface
  3-D, 79
  curved, 76
  model, 67
  modeling, 137
  solid, 64, 68
surface normals, 86
surface rendering *See* light
surfaces of revolution, 82 to 84
swept surface, 82
synthetic camera, 54
system level benchmark, 157

T

tablet, 23
Technical Interest Group for Performance
    Evaluation (TIGPE), 157

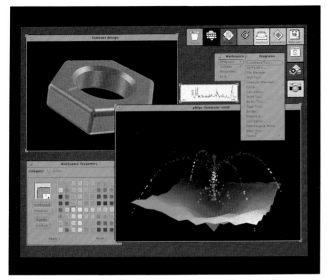

Color Plate 1 Application windows in the OPEN LOOK Graphical User Interface Environment.

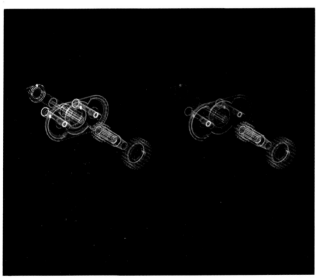

Color Plate 2 Depth-cued drill assembly, rendered on a Sun Microsystems SPARCstation 2GT. Image data and software courtesy of Parametric Technology Corporation.

Color Plate 3 An aliased image of an airplane, rendered on a Sun Microsystems SPARCstation 2GT. Image data courtesy of McDonnell-Douglas.

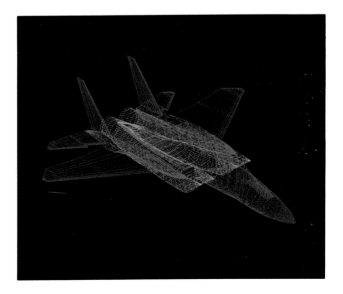

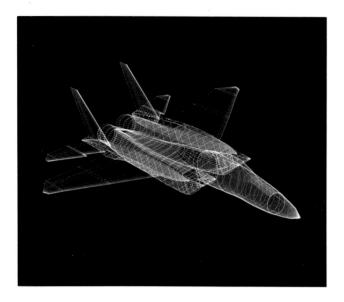

Color Plate 4 Antialiased airplane, rendered on a Sun Microsystems SPARCstation 2GT.   Image data courtesy of McDonnell-Douglas.

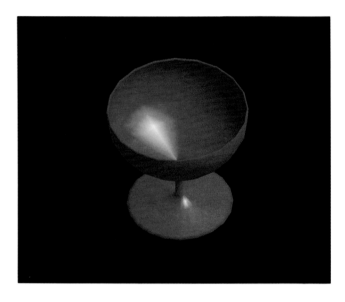

Color Plate 5 Gouraud-shaded goblet, rendered on a Sun Microsystems SPARCstation 2GT. Image data courtesy of Frank Crow.

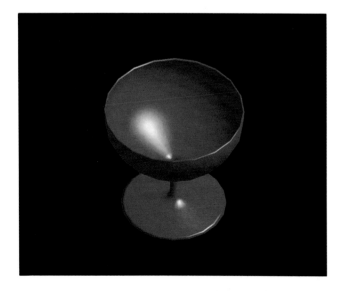

Color Plate 6 Phong-shaded goblet, rendered on a Sun Microsystems SPARCstation 2GT. Image data courtesy of Frank Crow.

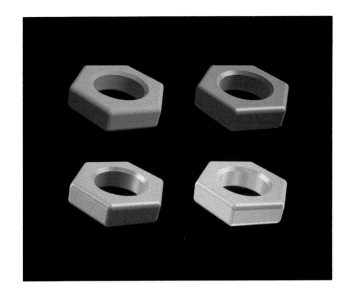

Color Plate 7 Mechanical part (nut) rendered with multiple light sources on a Sun Microsystems SPARCstation 2GT. Image data courtesy of Roger Day.

Color Plate 8 A ray-traced scene illustrating reflective and translucent objects. Ray tracing code developed by Kory Hamzeh.

Color Plate 9 An example of fluid flow dynamics, rendered with SunVision software on a Sun Microsystems VX application accelerator. The rendering reveals the location and structure of layers of fluids of different temperature ranges. Image data courtesy of Ballistic Research Labs.

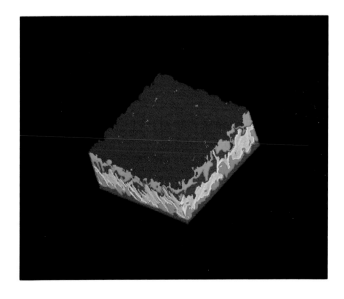

Color Plate 10 A sample image from an electronic publishing application. Image courtesy of Media Logic.

Color Plate 11 A sample image from an electronic computer-aided design application.

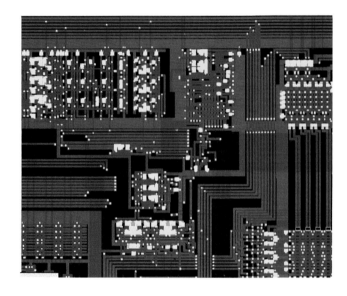

Color Plate 12 A sample image from an animation graphics application.

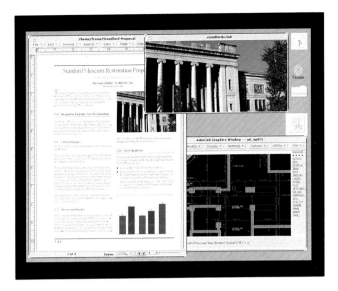

Color Plate 13 A sample image from an architecture, engineering, and construction application.

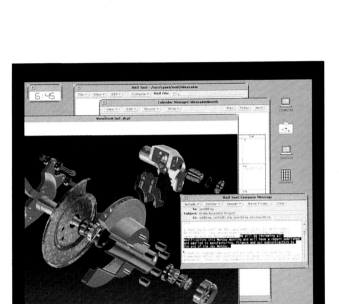

Color Plate 14 A sample image from a mechanical computer-aided design application. Image data courtesy of Structural Dynamics Research Corporation.

Color Plate 15 A sample image from a geographic information systems application. Image courtesy of Earth Resource Mapping Pty. Ltd.

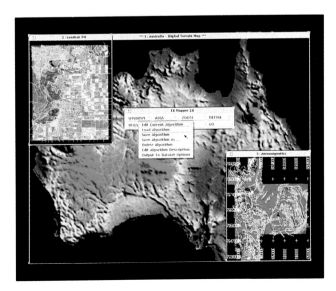

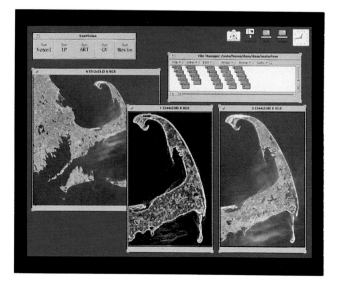

Color Plate 16 A sample image from an earth resources application.

Color Plate 17 A sample image from a medical imaging application.

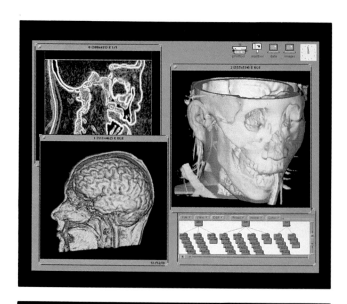

Color Plate 18 A sample image from a molecular modeling application.

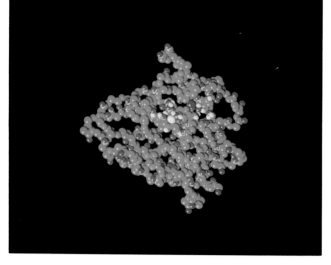

Please Return This Card

How did this book fit your needs?

☐ This book was useful to me.

The information in this book was: ☐ Detailed enough ☐ Too detailed

☐ Not detailed enough

User Type (Check all that apply) **:**

☐ End User ☐ VAR ☐ Consultant

☐ OEM ☐ Government ☐ University

☐ Developer ☐ System Administrator

My Applications are:

☐ Drafting/Mechanical Eng. ☐ Geographic Information Systems

☐ Electronic Design ☐ Architecture/Engineering/Constr.

☐ Image Processing ☐ Scientific Research/Visualization

☐ Earth Resources ☐ Desktop Publishing

☐ Pharm/Chem ☐ Color Prepress/Graphic Arts

☐ Medical ☐ Document Imaging

☐ Animation/Simulation ☐ Other _____

Graphics Product Interest:

☐ Hardware

☐ Software _____

What hardware and software are you currently using? _____

Purchase Plans:

☐ 0-2 months ☐ 7-12 months

☐ 3-6 months ☐ Budgeted

Buying: ☐ Make decisions ☐ Influence decisions ☐ Use system

☐ I would like Sun graphics product information. ☐ Hw. ☐ Sw.

☐ Please add me to your mailing list.

Name _____

Title _____

Company _____

Address _____

City, State, Zip _____

Telephone _____

☀ Sun
microsystems

ICGC 6/91

BUSINESS REPLY MAIL

FIRST CLASS   PERMIT NO. 1763   Denver, CO

POSTAGE WILL BE PAID BY ADDRESSEE

Sun Microsystems, Inc.
P.O. Box 5164
Denver, CO 80217-9343